From Pat and Jane
June 1, 2003
B day

SOLDIERS AT THE DOORSTEP

CIVIL WAR LORE

SOLDIERS AT THE DOORSTEP

CIVIL WAR LORE

LARRY S. CHOWNING

TIDEWATER PUBLISHERS
CENTREVILLE, MARYLAND

Library of Congress Cataloging-in-Publication Data

Chowning, Larry S., 1949–
   Soldiers at the doorstep : Civil War lore / by Larry S. Chowning.
  — 1st ed.
    p. cm.
  Includes index.
  ISBN 0-87033-519-7 (alk. paper)
  1. United States—History—Civil War, 1861–1865 Personal narratives.   2. United States—History—Civil War, 1861–1865—Social aspects Anecdotes.   3. Oral history.   I. Title.
E655.C48   1999
973.7'8—dc21   99-27180
                                                      CIP

Manufactured in the United States of America
First edition

To my mother and father

CONTENTS

PREFACE

The purpose of this project is not to address the great causes that led to one of the most destructive wars in American history—that has most certainly been done. This book has been written simply to provide a feeling, through oral history, of what life was like at home in tidewater Virginia during the years of the Civil War.

For much of the war, many areas of the South were behind enemy lines. Folks at home had to deal with the constant threat of Union soldiers arriving on their doorsteps. Much of what happened at home was not written down in history books, but some of it has been passed down by word of mouth.

Oral history is the very essence of all history. Let's face it, most written history starts out as oral history. Something happens, people talk about the happenings and events—oral history—and then it is written down. I have often had people ask me if I think stories people have told me have been embellished. I believe many of them have been, just as I believe many stories in the history books have been, too.

The stories in this book are southern tales. They have been passed down from slaves, Confederate soldiers, and women and children who were left at home to deal with the Yankee occupation.

These stories have been told many times as they were handed down from family member to family member.

Sometimes I reflect back to my own childhood and remember what was told to me as a child. I lived on Watling Street in Urbanna, Virginia, where my relatives and neighbors remembered those who fought in the war. I can still hear the force in my great-uncle's voice when he told me, "Don't ever forget where you have come from. You are a Virginian first and everything else thereafter." Today, kids would laugh at such a notion, but Charlie, who was born in 1889, was a product of the Civil War era. His father fought for General Robert E. Lee in the Army of Northern Virginia. It was a heart-breaking and emotional time for those living in the North and the South. Strong passionate feelings were often passed down from father to son and mother to daughter.

I have a feeling that the stories in this book are similar to stories that can be found throughout the rest of the South—wherever Union troops came and went. I also have a feeling that if a similar project were done in Pennsylvania, for example, where southern troops roamed, similar stories would be told of how northern civilians were treated and how they coped.

This project has taken years to do, but for most of those years I did not know that it was a project at all. It began when I was a child. My first recollections are of swinging on the front porch with my great-uncle at his home in late autumn. The chill of winter was in the air; I was wrapped in sweaters. My feet could not yet hit the floor and Charlie had rigged up a rope pull so he could pull the swing without using his feet. When we would get up high, he would yell, "Swingy, swingy," put his feet down on the floor, and I would crash to the floor. We didn't go so high that it would hurt me and when I crashed we would laugh and laugh. It wasn't long after this that Charlie began to pass our family stories down to me.

I do not remember a time, growing up, that the Yankee sword Charlie's father brought back from the war was not in the corner of the living room over by the fireplace. You don't ever remember not knowing your relatives because they were there when you first began to remember things. The sword was the same way.

Charlie wasn't the only one who had memories of the war. My next-door neighbor Cora Marchant loved history. I only knew her as Mrs. Marchant and it would be years before I would know that her first name was Cora. She had a Yankee cannonball that she kept underneath an American boxwood bush. For whatever reason, it always seemed to have moss growing on it. In the heat of the summer the ball was always moist and felt cool to my feet. When I was too young to know better, Mrs. Marchant told me that it was her cannonball that had killed the hare during the bombardment of Urbanna by Yankee gunboats. The legend is that Yankees bombarded the town for several hours and were only able to kill an old hare. It was some years later that I began to doubt it was *that* cannonball, but it made a good story and Mrs. Marchant could spin a good yarn.

Farther down the street lived Mrs. Ada Burton. I started delivering newspapers when I was eleven years old and would go by her house on Saturdays to collect my money. On several occasions, Mrs. Burton pulled out a Confederate five- or ten-dollar bill and offered it to me for payment. I recall once saying to her, "I can only take American money." She laughed and said, "This *is* American money." I have often wondered what she would have done if I had taken it.

For a short while my Uncle Carroll Chowning lived on Watling Street across from Mrs. Marchant's house. I remember him showing me the "Oath and Parole" papers signed by George W. Smith, my great-great-grandfather, on May 22, 1865. All Confederate soldiers were required to sign such a document and give their "faithful" allegiance to the United States of America. Uncle Carroll would later relate several family stories about the war to me. One of them, "The *Bloomer*," is in this book.

Bob and Elizabeth Bristow lived on the corner. One of their relatives, Captain Billy Christian, had dragged my great-grandfather from the battlefield after he was shot in the jaw by Yankees. So often the Bristows would invite me to sit with them on their side porch and they would share their memories. Some years later, when I was a man, Mrs. Bristow lay dying in her parlor. I went for a final visit, but when I arrived I didn't know what to say. I knew the end was near for her. And although her face was weathered with illness, the smile that was there so often for me when I was a child spread across her face. We talked for over an hour about riding bikes on summer days, swinging on the porch, picking blackberries, making Christmas cookies, and savoring the "diamonds of March"—the sun's sparkling reflections on the creek. She never mentioned her illness or her future. That was her way. Her strength and courage came to mind when I interviewed several people for stories in this project that related to southern women.

It was from these early experiences that a seed was planted in me that would eventually lead to this project. All of the people I mentioned above have gone to their Maker, but I remember each of them with fondness. Some years later, I also realized that I had lived in a very special time and place. Their lives and their stories have become an important part of my own life. I hope these stories will in some way touch you as well.

SOLDIERS AT THE DOORSTEP

DOORSTEP

CIVIL WAR LORE

1

THE *BLOOMER*

When I was eleven years old, my father bought me a 5½-horsepower Evinrude outboard engine. He put it on a twelve-foot flat-bottom wooden skiff and told me to go have fun, but be careful.

Suddenly, the world was opened up to me and that summer of 1960 is etched in my mind. My boat was more than just a means of catching gray trout, sugar toads, and ripe peelers. It became my ticket to a summer job.

My great-uncle Carroll Chowning, Sr., lived up the creek from us near Oak's Landing on Urbanna Creek. By land, I would have had to walk eight miles to get to his home, but by water it took less than a thimbleful of gas. Uncle Carroll asked my father if I wanted a summer job cutting his grass. He would supply the lawn mower and gas, and I could travel over in my boat. Dad was always interested in seeing me do something worthwhile, so he encouraged me to take the job. It was to be a summer that I would never forget. Uncle Carroll was a local historian of sorts and he knew a great deal about my family and its history.

Each week, I would cut his grass and when I was about halfway through, he would encourage me to take a break. He would bring down two ice-cold bottles of Coke, one for me and one for him. We would sit beneath the giant oaks not a stone's throw from the Glebe, the home place of my paternal great-great-grandparents and where my grandfather, Henry Shepherd Chowning, Sr., was born. There, Uncle Carroll would relate to me stories of my ancestors. At the time, I didn't realize he was passing the torch, and that one day I would be the one to relate his stories to others in my own family. This was one of the stories he told me on a hot July day in the summer of 1960, while drinking a cold Coke beneath the shade of a giant red oak.

The Glebe was located at the headwaters of Urbanna Creek. In colonial days it served as home for ministers of Christ Church parish in

3

Middlesex County. It was used by the Church of England from 1667 until the Revolution, when the English government and its Anglican church lost their power to the American victors.

After the American Revolution, the large square two-story brick Georgian house came under the control of the Overseers of the Poor and was for a short while used as a smallpox inoculation center.

Around 1814, the home and property ended up in the private sector, and in 1846, my great-great-grandfather George W. Smith purchased the Glebe. Uncle Carroll was born in 1884 to my great-grandparents, James Henry Chowning and Ann Eliza Smith Chowning. Ann Chowning was the daughter of George Smith. By 1864, the Smith household had felt the pain of war. Ann's father George, husband James, and brother William had all gone off to fight for Virginia and the Confederacy. In 1863, William was killed on the same night Stonewall Jackson received his fatal wounds at the battle of Chancellorsville.

One summer night in 1864, Ann Chowning, her mother, and a few slaves were all that were left at home to protect the Glebe. Union gunboats had been seen frequently on the Rappahannock River, and locals were constantly afraid the Yankees might attack their homes. On this summer night, a slave came running up to the main entrance of the Glebe and yelled for Miss Ann to come quickly.

A ship was sailing up the creek, but it had a Confederate flag atop the mast. Ann ran down to the shoreline to look for herself. Off in the distance, she could see the sailing vessel making its way up the creek.

"She's loaded down with something, Miss Ann," said the slave. "Look at her waterline." The vessel was low in the water.

Ann would learn later that the vessel was loaded with grain. Suddenly a faraway sound of cannons being fired could be heard. Ann ordered the slave to go back to the Glebe and fetch her father's spyglass. When the slave returned, she looked out and saw that the small Confederate vessel was being chased. A large Union ship that could go no farther upstream without running aground was trying in vain to sink the other boat with its cannons.

The captain of the Confederate vessel sailed his vessel as far upstream as the water depth would allow, and she came to rest in the mud of a cove right next to the Glebe.

Ann and her slave made their way over to the spot where the boat had stalled.

"Captain!" she shouted. "Can we help you?"

The vessel was named the *Bloomer* and was captained by a master sailor, Captain Hiram Carter.

"My name is Captain Hiram Carter, madam," he said. "I am in a bit of a dilemma here."

Just as he made that statement, a cannonball landed very nearby.

"I'm trapped but I will not let them take my ship."

Captain Carter and his mate had already made plans to stop the Yankees from taking the *Bloomer*. They had placed explosives on deck to blow her up.

"Madam, there are several things aboard I wish to save," he said. "Can your slave help us unload?"

"By all means," said Ann. "We will hide you and your items."

Captain Carter, his mate, and Ann's slave unloaded furniture and other belongings of importance to the captain.

Ann had another slave bring a horse and wagon to the shoreline, load up all the items, and carry them to the barn.

When all was off the boat, the captain and his mate went back aboard and set the ship afire. They rowed back to shore in the skiff and watched from the shoreline as the *Bloomer* went up in flames. When the explosives ignited, she went off like a Roman candle.

"Come Captain Carter. We will hide you," said Ann. "If the Yankees get up here, we will tell them their cannonballs killed you."

There was a place back in the woods dug into the side of a hill that George Smith had his slaves create. It was a hideout for his family in case the Yankees were to come. Ann and her slave led Carter and his mate to the spot.

For two days, the Smiths waited for the Yankees to come. On the evening of the second day, the crew aboard the Union ship hoisted sail and sailed away. Still, the Smiths and Captain Carter wondered if they would come back.

The captain and his mate hid in the hideout for two weeks. The Smiths fed them, watched over them, and had them up to the big house at night when they felt all was safe. There were only two ways into the Glebe: by water and by one road. Slaves were posted at both entrances.

After two weeks, Captain Carter told Ann's slave that he felt the Yankees would not come now and all was safe.

He went to the barn and pulled out an earthenware pitcher that had been saved from the *Bloomer*. The captain brought it to the house and gave it to Ann as a token of thanks.

After staying two weeks at the Glebe, Captain Carter gave Ann this brown earthenware pitcher as a token of his appreciation to her for helping him escape from the Yankees. The pitcher has remained in the Chowning family as a reminder of the Civil War days.

The Glebe was home to Ann Smith Chowning who gave refuge to the Confederate Captain Hiram Carter when Yankee ships chased the captain and his vessel the *Bloomer* to the headwaters of Urbanna Creek.

Carroll Chowning, Sr., shared this family story of Ann Smith Chowning, my great-grandmother, and Captain Hiram Carter, a Confederate sea captain, with me in 1960 when I was eleven years old. (Photo courtesy of Betty Chowning)

Captain Carter and his mate left the Glebe the next day but would return some months later to retrieve the rest of his possessions.

When Uncle Carroll had finished his story, he said to me, "Wait a minute. Before you go back to cutting grass, there's something I want to show you."

He went to the house and brought down that earthenware pitcher that Captain Hiram Carter had given my great-grandmother. "There she is," he said.

I held it for several minutes as my mind drifted back to the story he had just told me.

2

A SAFE PLACE

"Days before Appomattox, many battle-worn Confederates felt the end of the war was near. Some left the ranks and started for home. The Yankees also knew the end was near and wanted to make a final statement to the southern people and their lost cause. Yanks, with only one thing in mind—to find and kill as many Confederates as possible—stormed across the state.

"Now, I've seen nothing in the history books about this but there were some Yankees who were killing every white southern male who looked old enough to tote a rifle. Many teenage boys lost their lives by just being in the wrong place at the wrong time. . . ." said William Taliaferro, whose great-grandfather, William Jefferson Chapman of Isle of Wight County, Virginia, was nearly killed by the Yankees.

"Are the shades pulled, Mammy?" asked William Chapman.

"Yes sir, Massa William, you can go up and rest yourself now," said Mammy, a large black woman who was one of the house slaves for the Chapman family.

Mammy was very special to the Chapmans. She was born on the farm and very old by this time. She had been the midwife when William's father came into the world and had also helped William's mother when he was born sixteen years before.

The Chapman family had heard stories of what was happening in the war and knew Union troops were coming and going in the area. The Yankees would come into a neighborhood looking for

Confederate soldiers to kill. The problem was that not all the Yankees cared if the young men were a threat or not. Oftentimes, young white boys who had played no part in the war were being shot on sight because they looked old enough to have fought for the Confederacy.

To make matters worse for the Chapmans, William was big for his age. He looked to be eighteen or nineteen years old, and he and his family were constantly fearful that he would be taken by the Yankees and killed.

Anticipating that the Yanks might come onto the farm, the Chapmans had located several good places for him to hide. By day, William would stay hidden, and by night he would come home to eat and rest. The Chapman house was right far off the main road, and Mammy and others had made black shades to pull down over the windows so the light from the lamps could not be seen from the road.

During the night, William would go upstairs with the rest of the family and sleep while several slaves stood watch over the house.

On this particular morning, William had finished his breakfast and was about ready to leave for his hiding place when one of the slaves came running up to the porch yelling, "The Yankees are here! They're coming to the house!"

The women went into a panic, while William's first thought was to get to the barn or somewhere safe.

"No time, Massa William! They'll see you go to the barn. You best find a place in the house," said one of the slaves.

"You all, go on in the house," Mammy said to the white women.

She then turned to the other house slave and said, "Go in there and bring me that big basket of string beans that need snapping."

Mammy sat down in the rocking chair on the back porch and pulled up her dress and spread her legs wide. "Massa William, get under here right now or those Yankees are sure 'nuff going to kill ya."

William did not hesitate. He crawled up under her dress and she pushed it down so that it covered him completely. Then she started snapping string beans and singing a song.

The Yankees rode up to the front of the house. Several men went inside and dragged Mrs. Chapman and her daughters out into the yard. "Where are all your men?" asked the soldier in charge.

"They've all gone to war," answered Mrs. Chapman.

"Well, we're just going to see for ourselves, madam," said the soldier. "All right, boys. Let's find us some Johnny Rebs!"

The Yankees began searching the outbuildings and all around the property. They went down into the ravine where the Chapmans threw their trash and into the woods out beyond the pasture. While some were looking outside, others were looking through the house, barn, and outbuildings. One soldier walked over to Mammy. She never stopped snapping beans. He sat down on the step and took off his Yankee blue hat and laid it down beside him.

"Where are all the white boys, madam? I know they're around here somewhere," he said to Mammy. "This war will be over soon and you will be free to go anywhere you want. Nobody will bother you if you tell me where they're hid."

"I just don't know, massa. They all gone to war to kill you Yankees is all I know," said Mammy paying more attention to her work than the soldier.

Finally, all the soldiers came back to the house and informed their leader that they couldn't find anyone. "They're here somewhere," he said. "But we ain't got time to look anymore; let's move on to another place."

When they were gone, William came out from under Mammy's dress and he gave her a big hug. "Thank you, Mammy."

"Go on, boy. Did ya really think I was going to let those no-goods take ya and kill ya?" she said.

Although Mammy was freed after the war, she stayed on at the Chapmans' farm until she died. As a final tribute, she was buried in the Chapman family graveyard.

This story was told to William Taliaferro of Essex County by his uncle, Robert Ryland Taliaferro, who lived at Bray's Fork, Virginia. The family story had been passed down to him from his mother,

Daisy Chapman from Isle of Wight. She heard it from her father, William Jefferson Chapman, the boy who hid beneath Mammy's dress.

Bill Taliaferro of Montague Farms in Essex County.

BEHIND ENEMY LINES AND OTHER FAMILY STORIES

Atlee Steck told me these stories in 1997. They provide some insight into what life was like for those living behind enemy lines during the Civil War. Mrs. Steck's paternal and maternal ancestors were Confederates and lived in enemy-occupied territory on the north banks of the Rappahannock River in Falmouth and Hartwood. Atlee and her husband John were both born in homes that were built on the battlefields near Fredericksburg.

"My great-grandmother, great-great grandmother, and great-great-great-grandmother all lived in Falmouth behind Union lines. If you know the story of the battle of Fredericksburg then you know that Union forces occupied those heights on the riverbanks in Stafford County. Falmouth is on the Rappahannock River right across from Fredericksburg on the north bank.

"During the entire time the war was going on, the women in my family were the only ones at home. All the men were off fighting the war. The women living at home on my [maternal] grandfather's side were Elizabeth Bolling Dickens, born in 1811 [Mrs. Steck's great-great-great-grandmother]; Martha Anne Dickens Welsh, born 1829 [Mrs. Steck's great-great-grandmother]; and her daughter, my great-grandmother, Mary Frances Welsh Young. She was born in 1850. Throughout the war years, they lived alone there at the home place behind Yankee lines.

"My maternal grandmother's parents were Lathams and they lived in Hartwood, which was on Warrenton Road [later Route 17] about ten miles up the road from Falmouth. That's where that famous mud march took place when the Yankees tried to cross the Rappahannock at Kelly's Ford. The Yanks were going to try and come around Lee's army, and that's when [Stonewall] Jackson beat them at Chancellorsville. That was about 1863.

"Grandma [Harriett] Latham, as we called her, had a much rougher time of it than my relatives at Falmouth. [Grandma Latham was Mrs. Steck's great-grandmother.]

"The Yankees took everything she and her children had and left them without any food. She buried three of her young children before the war ended. They were babies and she didn't have enough food to keep them healthy. She had ten children altogether. The first one was born in 1857 and the last one was born in 1873. The last one was my grandmother. She had children born in 1859, 1860, 1861, 1864, and 1865. Three of those children died during the war and she had to bury them herself. She got some help from the other women in the neighborhood and from black people who were around, but you know it was a hard time for them.

"When Grandma Latham's husband, Thomas Latham, and some of his brothers did come home during the war, she would meet them out in the woods at a hiding place, because they weren't supposed to be behind Union lines. Their clothes and hair were full of lice. She had to boil their clothes and give them lye soap baths before they could come in the house. Maybe it would have been better if she had kept the lice on him [her husband] and then she wouldn't have had a child every year.

"I heard the old folks talk about how hungry the men were when they came home. They were nearly starved to death. There wasn't much at home for them to eat, though. The Yankees took what they wanted—the pigs, the cows. They took everything—the

Mary Frances Welsh Young, *left*, was Atlee Steck's great-grandmother. Frances, her mother, and her grandmother lived on the north bank of the Rappahannock River across from Fredericksburg behind Yankee lines throughout the war.

furniture from the house, everything. My people weren't big land-owners. They just had small farms.

"My grandmother, whose family was at Falmouth, used to say that they were better off living at Falmouth than the Lathams who were at Hartwood. The ones at Falmouth lived within the main supply line of the Yankee army. They were behind the Union lines too, but they had Union soldiers camped all around them and they would come to their house with cornmeal, bacon, and other food and ask the women to cook for them. They were being supplied directly from Washington. The Yankees would bring the supplies by train to Aquia and then cross over the Potomac by boat to Belle Plains. The bridges on the Potomac and Rappahannock rivers had both been blown up.

"The Yankees, who were camped all around, would come to my relatives' house at Falmouth and get the women to cook for them. In return, the women would take a little for themselves and in that way they would get something to eat. They lived right at Falmouth Heights where the main camp for the Yankees was located. The [Rappahannock] river is not that wide up there. Right on the other side of the river you had the entire Confederate forces. They didn't have anything hardly to eat, so my relatives were better off than they were. I can hardly believe that that little Rappahannock River separated those two big armies. If you lived in Falmouth, Fredericksburg was just like living in a foreign county.

"I remember hearing some of the men in my family criticize those women. They would say they could not understand why those three women had to take food from the Yankees. But I always said that hunger will make you do a lot of things, and if I was hungry and someone brought me cornmeal and bacon, I would be happy to eat it. I think they were very brave women.

"There is no question that my ancestors at Falmouth hated the Yankees. They hated them with a terrible passion."

Mrs. Steck pulled out an old family photo album. "Let me show you something. This picture of John Wilkes Booth should tell you something. They thought he was a fine man. He was a hero to them, but can you imagine having a photograph of him today in your family album?" she asked, shaking her head.

"I do remember a story passed down by my mother. Long after the war was over, these old Union veterans would come back every few years and have a big reunion either for the Battle of Chancellorsville, the battle of the Wilderness, or the battle of Salem Church. It was the same time that they put two or three of those big monuments out on Plank Road [later Route 3].

"Now this was when my mother was a girl and it's about my mother's grandmother, who had lived behind the Union lines at Hartwood. She would forbid any of her children or grandchildren to even go in the yard if any of those Yankees were on the street. One day my great-aunt went out in the yard and started flirting with the Yankees. They would say something like, "Can I have a rose out of your yard?" My great-grandmother came out and chased her in the house and forbid her to speak to anyone who even looked like a Yankee.

"Another family story that was passed down was that, after the war, there wasn't a tree left in Stafford County because the Yankees camped there and burned all the trees up in the thousands and thousands of camp fires. So, after the war, in 1867 great-grandmother Latham and her husband moved off the farm because there was no wood to burn in the stove. They moved to Fredericksburg, into the old Rising Sun Tavern. That's where they lived when my grandmother was born.

"My great-grandfather died in 1872 and my great-grandmother wanted to take him back to the Hartwood Presbyterian Church cemetery to be buried, but the roads were still torn up from the war. He died December 30 and it was almost spring before they could get him to Hartwood. The roads were just totally destroyed from the war. You couldn't get the horses to pull the wagon with the casket on it through all the mud and muck. They didn't have ice then so I don't know how they kept him. Maybe it was just a cold winter. Later, I went up there to try and find his tombstone and other things concerning my family. Well, there are no records. The Yankees

Mary Frances Welsh Young standing in front of what is believed to be her home at Hartwood, Virginia. During the Civil War, the main Yankee armies camped in her yard and on the surrounding property.

This old faded photo of John Wilkes Booth was found in the Welsh family photo album by Atlee Steck. She said that Booth was a hero to her Virginia ancestors. "Can you imagine having a photo of John Wilkes Booth in your family album today?" she asked.

burned up everything everywhere they went. There are no records in Stafford County prior to the Civil War.

"When John and I were grade-school children, they held the first reenactment of the battle of Chancellorsville. The VMI boys were the Confederates. The governor was there. It was a big deal. The Union army was made up of marines from the Quantico marine base. The most memorable thing that I recall was when the Yankees were in the Wilderness, and all those VMI cadets started singing 'Old Joe Hooker Come Out of the Wilderness.' This was a big impression on a kid. I knew all about the war because I'd heard my great-grandparents and grandparents talk about it—mainly my grandparents because they were born shortly after the war. They carried on about it. In Fredericksburg, Memorial Day was as big a day as the Fourth of July and Washington's Birthday are now. The national guard and the color guard from Quantico would march in a parade and all the schoolchildren would march to the Confederate cemetery and put roses on the graves of the Confederate dead. We would not have put a flower on a Yankee grave for anything.

"The people who supported the Union army would march on out to the national cemetery and put flowers on the Yankee graves. None of us schoolchildren ever went out to the national cemetery. Even when we were coming along, I'm seventy-two and John is seventy-four [in 1997], I can't believe that when we were children that we would have even considered putting a rose or a flower on a Union grave. Getting ready for the Memorial Day parade at school, we would practice for weeks singing, 'The Bonnie Blue Flag.'

"Because Fredericksburg and Stafford were so immersed in the battles, the hatred and ill feelings towards the North carried on into us. We were the third generation after the war.

John and Atlee retired to Urbanna, Virginia, in 1983 and brought with them memorabilia passed down from their relatives who survived the war. Perhaps the most interesting treasure is a written recollection from John's relatives, who recount a story that was told to them by their mother and great-aunt. Signed by

FREDERICKSBURG, VA.
May 11th, 1909.

VISIT OF

15th REGIMENT

OF

New Jersey Volunteer Veterans

PROGRAMME

Col. E. D. Cole, Chairman.

Music,	Prof. Franklin's Orchestra
Address,	Mayor H. Lewis Wallace

Introducing Hon. John T. Goolrick, who delivers
Welcome Address.

Music,	By Orchestra

Response to Address of Welcome,

Hon. John Franklin Fort, Governor of New Jersey

Song,	"America"
Voluntary Address,	By Veterans
Music,	By Orchestra
Song,	"Star Spangled Banner"

America.

My country! 'tis of thee,
Sweet land of liberty,
  Of thee I sing;
Land where my fathers died!
Land of the pilgrims' pride!
From every mountain side
  Let freedom ring!

My native country, thee,
Land of the noble free,
  Thy name I love;
I love thy rocks and rills,
Thy woods and templed hills;
My heart with rapture thrills
  Like that above

Let music swell the breeze,
And ring from all the trees
  Sweet freedom's song.
Let mortal tongues awake;
Let all that breathe partake;
Let rocks their silence break,
  The sound prolong.

Our fathers' God! to Thee,
Author of liberty,
    To Thee we sing;
Long may our land be bright
With freedom's holy light;
Protect us by Thy might,
    Great God, our King!

The Star-Spangled Banner.

Oh, say, can you see by the dawn's early light,
    What so proudly we hailed at the twilight's
        last gleaming,
Whose broad stripes and bright stars, thro'
        the perilous fight,
    O'er the ramparts we watched, were so
        gallantly streaming?
And the rockets' red glare, the bombs burst-
        ing in air,
Gave proof thro' the night that our flag was
        still there.

CHORUS.

Oh, say, does that star-spangled banner yet
        wave
O'er the land of the free and the home of the
        brave?

Oh, thus be it ever when freeman shall stand
    Between their loved home and wild war's
        desolation;
Blest with victory and peace, may the heaven-
        rescued land
    Praise the Power that hath made and pre-
        served us a nation!
Then conquer we must, when our cause it is
        just,
And this is our motto: "In God is our trust!"

CHORUS.

And the star-spangled banner in triumph shall
        wave
O'er the land of the free and the home of the
        brave.

Once the war was over, Confederate and Union veterans held reunions in the Fredericksburg area. This program from a 1909 reunion of the Fifteenth Regiment of the New Jersey Volunteers was found by Mrs. Steck in some of her relatives' belongings.

Josephine and Helen Steck, it describes that horrid night in Ford's Theater when Booth shot President Abraham Lincoln.

"For two little girls from Middletown, Maryland, ages nine and twelve years respectively, attending boarding school in Washington, D. C., this night of Good Friday, April 14, 1865, was to be a momentous occasion. They were looking forward to it with great enthusiasm, for as a special treat as part of their Easter vacation they were being taken to see the famous actor John Wilkes Booth in the outstanding play 'Our American Cousin' at Ford's Theater on 10th Street. Also there were exciting rumors afloat that the president might attend and they would have a chance to see him, too.

"Filled with excitement and eagerness for their first real theater experience, they had no thought for the tragedy soon to engulf them. As they told the story to us children in later years, they, along with their aunt and uncle accompanying them, were so stunned by the shots and events that followed, they seemed to sit in shock while pandemonium broke out all around them. People were screaming, running, climbing over each other in a mad rush to escape. Children were knocked down and trampled, and they in a mad rush lost their shoes and most of their clothing as it was torn from them. Too young to realize the magnitude of events, they thought at first that the shots and the leap of the assassin to the stage were part of the play but reality soon forced them to join the mad rush to get out. Somebody yelled, 'Stop that man!' Then a woman, later identified as Mrs. Lincoln, leaned over the box railing, shouting 'Help! Help! Help!' By the time our little girls and their escorts got out of the building, men were carrying President Lincoln across the street to the house where he later died.

"Those two little girls were our mother and Aunt Delia."

4

TALES FROM SLAVE TIMES

Nesting Plantation is located on the south side of the Rappahannock River in Jamaica District in Middlesex County, Virginia. The first patent on this land goes back to March 13, 1649, when Richard Perrott patented 450 acres.

The old house built by the Perrotts still stands, and a portion of it is said to have been built around 1655. It is believed to be the oldest house standing in Middlesex County. By the time of the Civil War, Nesting belonged to Mr. and Mrs. Joseph C. Eubank.

The Eubanks purchased the plantation (composed of 1,048 acres) and slaves in 1849. The family owned the plantation for nearly seventy years.

Several ancestors of Nesting slaves still live in the neighborhood and have shared with me short accounts of what life was like during slave times.

William B. Dickerson and Clemon Brown had grandparents who were slaves at old Nesting before and during the war. Their stories have been passed down to William and Clemon through their parents and grandparents. Also, Sherman Holmes shared a written account of his memories passed down from his grandparents who were slaves in Lancaster and Middlesex counties.

The first story would be considered racist by today's standards. However, it is important to understand from a historical standpoint that attitudes tell us a great deal about the way life was. It should be understood that there is good and bad in history and as a society we should glean the good from each generation and leave the bad behind us.

A Look at Heaven

"When I was a little boy, my mother told me this story one night. It sounds almost like a joke, but she told me that this really happened and I believe her," recalled William Dickerson.

"During the war, Mrs. Eubank would oftentimes get depressed and she would sit on the front porch for hours. The house slaves would look after her, fanning her, and they would try to cheer her up.

"Days went by and she became more and more depressed with news that the Yankees were winning the war. One morning out of nowhere, Mrs. Eubank came bounding down the stairs all in a glow.

"The slaves were happy to see her so jolly and all the house slaves came onto the front porch to see what had made her so happy. There was an old slave named Mr. Jack there who had been on the plantation long before the Eubanks purchased Nesting. Mr. Jack was nearly ninety years old and had been born on the plantation. His people were some of the first slaves on the place, going all the way back to the Perrotts in the 1600s.

"After the Perrotts, the Corbins bought the place in the 1750s, and his people were owned by them. The Corbins owned the place for nearly a hundred years, and Mr. Jack had been a slave for the Corbins. The Browns [Jane and Christopher] bought the place in 1847 and Mr. Jack was still there. Then came the Eubanks and the war, and he was still on the plantation.

"Mr. Jack was very old now. He was bent over, white-haired, and hard of hearing. He was about ready to go to his Maker. Mrs. Eubank tried to prepare her slaves for death. She believed that it was important that her slaves be in heaven when she got there.

"Mr. Jack asked Mrs. Eubank what had happened that night that had made her so happy, and she told him that she had seen heaven in a dream and that it was wonderful.

"She told of a beautiful plantation where life was always happy and there was no pain.

"The old slave's eyes perked up and he moved closer to hear about heaven. 'Mrs. Eubank, tell me: Did you see any colored people in heaven?' he asked.

" 'No, Jack, I did not, but I didn't go back to the kitchen,' she answered."

Emancipation at Nesting

"I don't know exactly when Mr. [Joseph] Eubank got around to telling us that the war was over and we were free, but my grandmother told my mother about the day we got the news," said Dickerson.

Old Nesting Plantation was home to hundreds of slaves from the mid-1600s to the time when freedom came in 1865. Built about 1649, it is believed to be the oldest house still standing in Middlesex County, Virginia. Several ancestors of Nesting slaves still live in the area and recall stories from those times.

"Master Eubank came riding down toward the slave shanties just before time to go into the fields. He was riding his best horse and he was dressed up, like he was going to church.

"He told one of the slaves that he wanted to talk to everyone and for all to come out. We all came out and he said, 'Well, you are all free. The war is over and we lost. You can go or you can stay. If you stay, you can live in your houses and I'll give each family a cow. I want the first calf from the cow and you can have the second. I want the third and you can have the fourth and so on.'

"With that, Master Eubank got on his horse and rode away. Most of the slaves stayed.

"We didn't yell or cheer. My grandmother said everyone just stood there for a while, looking around at one another because they didn't understand what it meant for them to be free."

A Slave Gun

As boys growing up in the Nesting area, William Dickerson and Clemon Brown heard the story of the four rifles that were given to the most trusted slaves on the Eubank plantation. Their task was to warn the Eubanks when Yankees were coming and to protect them from attack. After the war and after freedom came, the guns were dearly valued within the black community and today one still remains in the Nesting area. Dickerson's father purchased the gun in 1937 for twenty-five dollars from a relative of Charlie Smith, one of the four trusted slaves.

"There were four of these guns given out to the most trusted slaves on the plantation by their owner, Joseph Eubank," said Dickerson. "The rifles were all made at Harpers Ferry, West Virginia, in 1833, and each slave was given one and told to carve his name in the stock."

On the stock of Dickerson's gun the name "C. Smith" is roughly carved in the wood. The other sentries were Henry Stokes, John Wash, and Billy Burrell. "It was their job to be looking for Yankees and to let the folks on the plantation know that danger was coming," said Brown. "They were to keep anyone from invading the plantation. There were four stations for the sentries. They were po-

William B. Dickerson, *left,* and Clemon Brown hold a slave gun from old Nesting plantation. Slave owner Joseph C. Eubank issued four rifles to his most trusted slaves during the Civil War in an effort to protect the plantation near Jamaica, Virginia, from Yankee attack.

sitioned at Big Gate [the main entrance to Nesting], the entrance to Mud Creek, at Percifull Landing, and at The Point, which is on Parrotts Creek.

"To our knowledge, Nesting was never invaded by Yankees, but they were coming and going up and down the Rappahannock River all the time," said Dickerson.

"When Mr. Eubank told his slaves they were free to go, he did not ask for the rifles back, and the guns were used regularly for hunting. Many families would have starved in the winter if the community had not had those guns," he said.

When Dickerson's father purchased the rifle in 1937 it had not been fired for many years, so a group of men, all descendants of slaves from Nesting, decided to fire the gun for old time's sake. Dickerson was a small boy at the time, but he remembers that day with great humor. "They didn't know how to load it and no one wanted to hold it when it went off, so Ed Stokes got the bright idea that they should tie it to a tree and pull the trigger.

"Uncle George Lomax told us kids to run and we all took off for cover. Uncle George was old, but he beat us and that straight-legged beagle dog of his to the house," laughed Dickerson.

"The gun misfired and the group was satisfied that they had tried their hardest. They gave up on the idea of shooting the gun," said Dickerson.

Fanning Flies

"William Walker, my maternal grandfather, was born a slave on the Muse Farm near Towles Point in Lancaster County, Virginia," re-

Roughly carved in the stock of the rifle is the name "C. Smith" for Charlie Smith, one of the slaves given a rifle by slave owner Joseph C. Eubank. Today, the gun belongs to William B. Dickerson, the grandson of one of Nesting's slaves.

calls Sherman Holmes. "We do not know the exact date of his birth other than grandfather said that he was born in February nine years before the Civil War began. That would put the year of his birth about 1852. His mother's name was Eliza, and his father was a white man. Eliza had several sisters, and their children all lived on Muse's Farm. The sisters' names were Mary and Martha, who were twins, and Marie Louisa.

"Grandfather's job during the summer months was to fan flies from Master Muse's face and to take care of the cows all year long. Grandfather stated that when the Yanks stormed upon the Muse's farm, his aunt Louisa came in and said, 'Master Muse, the Yanks are here on the farm.'

"Old man Muse jumped up and ran to hide in the woods. Grandfather said he ran so fast that he fanned his own flies that day.

"Life on the Muse's farm was not so good at times. According to grandfather, young slave boys did not wear trousers until they were eight or nine years old. They wore a garment somewhat like a very long shirt which they pulled over their heads. It was made that way so that it did not take them long to dress. When slave boys were called to arise from their night's sleep, they could dress in a hurry. Also, they did not wear shoes until they were men. He said many were the days that he made the cows get up from their sleeping places so he could warm his feet in the places where the cows had slept.

"Grandfather, his mother Eliza, her three sisters, and others were personal slaves of one of the Muse's daughters who married a Mr. Segar in Middlesex County. This Mr. Segar purchased Grimsby, which was later named Wood's Farm in Middlesex. After the wedding, her slaves were transported across the river to Rosegill on a raft that was made for that purpose. They stayed at Rosegill for a long period of time while Grimsby was being made ready to be occupied. Grandfather said that Yankee gunboats came to Urbanna, which was across the creek from Rosegill. The young slave boys would swim out to the boats. They were given food and the sailors would throw coins into the water to see if they could dive to the bottom and retrieve them. If they could get a coin, they could keep it.

"The little band of slaves stayed on at Grimsby until they were freed. Some of them worked there for wages after freedom.

"Grandfather married a young girl by the name of Lucy Jane Lockley. My grandmother never knew her mother or father. She was told by her aunt Julia Wormeley and another lady by the name of Jane King that her father and mother had been sold to different people. Her mother was sold to someone in Georgia and she never knew where her father went. She was raised by Aunt Jane King on Deer Chase Farm, and after freedom came she lived in the King's Neck community which had been established by Lewis King, a free man of color. She never went to school, but she did learn to read and write."

5

CONFEDERATE HIP BOOTS
AND OTHER STORIES

Swainson Hudgins, eighty-seven, lives in New Point, Mathews County, Virginia, in the very house in which he was born. After he told me his story about Confederate hip boots, we walked to the edge of Dyer Creek behind his two-story wood clapboard house and he showed me where he took his first wade out into the water in his brand-new boots. We walked back to his house and he said, "I got a few more stories, too."

Christmas Boots

"My granddaddy, I called him Pa, was born in 1827. When I was five or six [around 1917], he was near on ninety years old. Pa was still working the water then and he would carry me along in his boat. I didn't go to school much even when I got old enough. While he worked, I'd be in the boat watching or playing. He'd carry along a rope and he'd tie it around my leg. If I fell overboard, he'd grab the rope and pull me back.

"I was around watermen all the time and you know how kids are; they want to be like grown people. When people get old, they want to be like young people. It's just the way people are. I'd see men in hip boots and I wanted a pair, but they didn't make hip boots

33

smaller than a size 6. You could get other types of boots in sizes 2 and 3, but not hip boots.

"I kept on growing and kept on growing, and finally I got to a size where I could fit into a pair. I got me a pair for Christmas. They were PAC Ballban. The trademark was a white cross with a little red ball. You may have seen them—if you're old enough.

"Anyway, great day-a-morning, I had my boots. I put them on on Christmas morning and I thought I could wade across the Bay—all the way across the Bay! It was a cold morning when I went down to the creek and waded on out to see what they felt like. They felt good too.

"That day we had a big Christmas dinner. I wore those boots all day. After dinner, all of us were in the parlor, sitting around talking, when Pa called me over to him. He grabbed me with that big hand of his and hugged me up close. He said to me, 'Let me tell you about the first boots I ever had. I was nearly a man when I bought me my first pair of boots. They were leather boots. Do you know what I paid for them?'

"I didn't know what to say because all Pa's boots were practically worn out. They had holes all into them. He didn't care because he could stand as much cold as an otter.

"I said, 'No sir.' You had to say yes sir and no sir back then or you would get your fanny spanked.

"Everybody around the room was guessing twenty cents or maybe a dollar. Finally he said, 'Ain't none of you close. I paid three hundred dollars for them boots.'

"Everybody looked around at each other. I mean, nobody wanted to call Pa a liar, but hell, in those days three hundred dollars was a half a year's wages. He would have bought those boots back during the war and it was tighter times than what we had then. I couldn't believe Pa *had* three hundred dollars, much less that he paid that much for a pair of leather boots.

"Finally, I said, 'Pa you're crazy.'

"He laughed and said, 'I paid three hundred dollars in Confederate money for those boots. The most expensive boots I ever owned.' We all laughed.

"It must have taken a whole lot of Confederate money to buy much back then. The money must not have been worth a damn."

Turtle Blood

"Pa didn't fight in the war. He was old enough but he didn't want to go so he would hide out in the woods and swamps all day to keep from being found by the Yankees and the Confederates. He would stay out in the woods in daytime, and at nighttime he would go sleep in a shack. The name of the place he would hide was called Grape Bush because there was grape vines all over it.

"He said he would eat anything he could find. He would go up to the top of trees and pick chestnuts and chinquapin nuts—all

Swainson Hudgins recalls stories that his ninety-year-old grandfather told him in 1917 about life in Mathews County during the Civil War.

kinds of wild fruit and nuts the old people had to live on in those days.

"Pa told me the Yankees would come around and steal and break up everything they could find. They would even break up our brine pots. Most everybody had cast-iron pots that were used to boil salt water in, and when the water evaporated out it would leave salt in the bottom of the pot. That's the way the old people around here got salt. There were brine holes over on the inside of the beach and they'd go over there and get the brine, put it in the pots, boil it, and pretty soon they had salt.

"So, the Yankees would go around and break up all these pots. They did anything to make life harder on us. But the old people knew how to fix the pots. This is hard to believe but I know Pa told me the truth. We got two or three kinds of turtles around home, but we got a little turtle called a green fin turtle that don't grow very big. Pa told me that the old people would catch a green fin turtle, cut its head off, and collect the blood. They would mix the blood with lime and take the mixture, coat pots with the mixture, to patch it. He said after that the pots were as good as new."

Confederate Guerrilla

"All up the Piankatank River was Yankee grounds. They had warships up there and Pa's brother was what you called a guerrilla. His name was Shad Hudgins. He and a bunch of boys would row up to the Yankee boats at night, sneak aboard, and kill as many Yankees as they could. I just can remember him. He was a real tall man and meaner than a junkyard dog.

"One night, they rowed up to a Yankee ship and got up on deck. There was a guard standing watch. He came at Shad with a sword. Shad took his own sword and cut the guard's head off just like he was cutting a watermelon. They robbed the boat, killed everyone they could, and set the boat afire."

6

BAPTIZED

"A lot of old people were not allowed to worship. I'm talking about slave times now. This is hard to say, but a lot of white people didn't want black people to know anything about God or anything else.

"There were good whites, though, wives of masters who would not tell their husbands about what we were doing, because they loved us and felt compassion for us," said Clemon Brown.

"I don't want none of them going to church, or you reading the Bible to them, or them being baptized! Now do you understand what I'm saying? We've never fought over much, but I'm not going to allow it!" screamed Joseph Eubank, owner and master of Nesting Plantation in Middlesex County, Virginia.

"Joe, the other slave owners around are allowing their slaves to hold services on the grounds as long as there is at least one white at the meeting," said Lucy Eubank, Joe's wife. "The slaves at Corbin Hall go to Glebe Landing [Baptist Church] every Sunday and sit up in the balcony. You know that. Don't you think we ought to help these people find God?"

Lucy was Joseph Eubank's second wife. His first wife had died of consumption, and Lucy had married him a year or so later. She was from Laneview, not far from Nesting. Her father had been one of the early Baptists who fought hard for religious freedom and was opposed to the institution of slavery.

Joe Eubank would ordinarily never have considered marrying a woman coming from such a family, but Lucy had striking good looks and she caught Joe's eye when she was just a young girl: she was still a teenager when Joe, in his midforties, proposed to her.

"Lucy, you knew I owned slaves when you came here," he said. "I control the slaves and you got nothing to do with them. They ain't going to church. They ain't going nowhere except in the fields and where I tell 'em to go."

Lucy Eubank was an attractive woman, with steel blue eyes, sandy blond hair, and a girlish figure that was still very much intact. She was usually quiet and appeared to be shy to many people. Her marriage to Joe had not been approved by her father, who felt that anyone who owned slaves was fit for nothing. Lucy married Joe anyway. "Love conquers all," she had told her mother.

The issue of slaves attending church was the first real fight that Joe and Lucy had had during their short marriage. Joe had agreed to leave the Anglican church and join the Baptists at Glebe Landing. Although he was not much of a religious man, when he found out that slaves attended Glebe Landing he had a fit.

He and several others paid to have an outside door installed on the side of the church. It led up to the balcony and was referred to as the slave door. "They ain't coming in the same door that I come in," he grumbled.

Once Joe had gone, Lucy flopped down into a chair. Judy, her house slave, had heard the conversation. "Judy, come here," said Lucy. Judy was a large woman in her seventies. She had been born on Nesting when the Corbins owned the plantation. When they sold to the Browns and then to the Eubanks, she and many other slaves went with the sale of the property.

"Has Joe always been this hardheaded?" Lucy asked.

"Ever since I known him," said Judy. "You can't do nothing with him. Shoot, girl, you've done more with Massa Joe than any woman has. You at least got him to go to church on Sunday. You got what it takes to make a man do what you want," said Judy with a grin.

"Oh, come on, Judy," said Lucy, blushing. Then her mood changed. "Judy, do you know about Jesus?" asked Lucy.

"I know what has been told me."

"What have you been told?"

"That there is a paradise in the sky that we all go to whether we is black or whether we is white," she said.

"Who told you that, Judy? Don't be scared to tell me. I won't tell Joe."

"Lordy, girl, I ain't scared of Massa Joseph or anyone else," said the slave. "The chairbackers, they're telling us about Jesus." ["Chairbacker" was a slave term for a black layman who preached the word of God.]

"The slaves come over here from Corbin Hall and they tell us about Jesus. Their massa allows them to go to church," said Judy. "They're telling us about Jesus, and they say we need to be baptized."

Lucy was quiet for a moment and then she said, "I want every slave on the place to be baptized."

"Massa Joseph won't have it," said Judy. "I know him. He's just like Massa Brown: hardheaded and stubborn! I've told him so, too—Massa Joseph won't hurt me because his father told him on his deathbed to look out after Judy and Simon."

Simon had been Judy's husband and had come to Nesting from Joe's father's place in Essex County. The slaves called Joe's father Massa Dan, and Simon was his favorite. When Simon died, his body was carried back to the farm in Essex to be buried very close to Massa Dan. A special cross made of hickory was erected to mark his grave.

"Ol' Massa Dan loved Simon because he was so good with horses," continued Judy. "Simon won a race at court day with Massa Dan's best filly. He even beat Massa Corbin's best stallion," she said with a laugh. "That's what Massa Dan really liked."

"Judy, do you know any of those chairbackers?" Lucy asked.

"Yeah, I know 'em, but I won't tell you who they are."

"I don't want to know who they are," said Lucy. "Do you think you can get them to come here and baptize the slaves?"

"What you thinking about?" Judy asked.

"I want you to find out when they can come, and I'll occupy Joe long enough so everyone here can be baptized."

"What about mean old Massa Harvey?" asked Judy.

Harvey Stubs was the slave master on the Eubanks' farm and had been for years. He would do whatever Joe Eubank told him to do.

"I see that Betty Mae has been part of some of Harvey's work lately," said Lucy. "That sweet baby girl she had several months ago wasn't all black."

Judy laughed. "And I thought you were innocent," she said. "Harvey sneaks out most every night from his wife's bed," said Judy. "Massa Joe has known it for years, but he don't care. It just means more slaves for him."

Lucy shook her head in disgust.

"Judy, you find out what night the chairbackers can come and we'll take care of Massa Joe and Harvey," said Lucy.

A season came and went before Judy got back to Lucy. It was summer and it had been a hot one at that.

Judy watched on this morning for Joe to go and see to the farm, and then she came from the kitchen. "The chairbackers can come Sunday night," she said to Lucy. "They say they can baptize us all down in the marsh near the millpond spillway."

"Are the slaves aware of what is happening?" asked Lucy.

"They know, but what are you going to do about Massa Joe and Harvey?"

"Come on, let's go down to the wine cellar," said Lucy.

The two went down to the cellar and picked a couple of bottles. "I want some of the best rum for Joe and the worst white lightning on the place for Harvey," said Lucy. "I want Harvey to feel real bad when he wakes up on Monday morning.

"Judy, you tell Betty Mae I want Harvey to be in her bed while all this is going on and tell her this jug of moonshine is to help keep him there."

"I'll give her the moonshine, but she won't need no help keeping him there," said Judy.

"You also tell her that when my father comes next month to see me, we'll sneak her down to the brook and I'll have him baptize her. And Judy, I want my white cotton nightgown pressed and ready for me Sunday night," she said.

"But that cotton gown is so hot. It's summertime."

"Sam loves that white gown and when the light is right you can see right through it. It drives him crazy," Lucy said and winked at Judy.

"Lordy, girl, with that figure ain't a man alive who could resist ya," said Judy with a big smile on her face. "This might end up being a family night for you and Massa Joe."

"Go on," said Lucy.

Judy laughed again.

At suppertime on Sunday night, Judy and the other slaves fixed up a big meal for Lucy and Joe. Lucy had the slaves take over some food to Stubs's household.

The baptism was to take place when the lights went out in Joe and Lucy's bedroom and in Betty Mae's shanty. Slaves were stationed so they could see the lights in the windows. If a light were to come back on, everything was to stop and the slaves were to go back to their shanties.

After supper, Joe had a couple drinks of rum and along about nine o'clock Lucy told him, "I'm going up to bed, love. Are you coming?"

"I'll be up after one more drink," he said.

Lucy went upstairs and put on her nightgown and unbraided her hair so that it dropped down below her waist.

She could hear Joe coming up the stairs, and when he opened the door she jumped into his arms and kissed him on the mouth and neck and then reached to unbutton his shirt.

Joe kissed her again and again.

"What's gotten into you tonight?" Joe asked as Lucy unbuttoned the front buttons on his pants.

Joe helped her pull her nightgown over her head and he grabbed her naked body. With her arms around his neck and his around her girlish waist, they lowered onto the bed.

"Cut the lamp out, Joe" she said. "I want this moment to last forever."

This story was passed down to Clemon by his grandmother, Judy Brown, who was a slave on the old Nesting farm. Clemon died in 1998, but several of his stories of slave times have been saved and are in this volume.

When Clemon finished telling me his story of how Joseph Eubank's slaves were baptized, he wept, and before the interview was over I was crying too. One of the last things he said to me that day was, "Now you see why church and Jesus mean so much to Bessie and me."

Clemon and his wife, Bessie, were two of the kindest, most decent, God-fearing people that I have ever met. This chapter is dedicated to their memory.

7

SAVING THE TAVERN

The following story about saving the tavern at King and Queen Courthouse has been told and retold around country stores of rural King and Queen County since it happened in 1864. I was first told the story by teacher and historian Louise Gray, formerly of King and Queen County. I'm well aware that many others have related this story from time to time. Thanks to all of those who have contributed to saving this tidbit of Civil War lore for posterity.[*]

King and Queen County's tavern is the oldest building still standing in the courthouse area at King and Queen Courthouse. When Yankees burned the courthouse and other buildings, the tavern was spared because of some quick thinking by local residents.

In 1864, the Union army under Brigadier General Judson Kilpatrick, commander of the Army of the Potomac Cavalry, planned a raid on the Confederate capital of Richmond. The purpose of the raid was to free Union officers and soldiers who were being held captive at Belle Isle and Libby prisons. The raiders included the forces of Colonel Ulric Dahlgren. The plan called for Kilpatrick to

---

[*] Some dates and names came from the August 4, 1983, article in the *Southside Sentinel* written by Robert Mason entitled "Special Civil War Maneuver Saved K & Q's Old Tavern."

move down from the north and Dahlgren to move up from the south and both would attack Richmond together.

As the Yankees moved toward Richmond in February 1864 they ran into strong resistance from the home front. Kilpatrick's forces were able to escape the area and move back down the peninsula to Gloucester Point and Yorktown, which by then was under Union control. Dahlgren's forces tried to cross the James River west of Richmond, actually got within two miles of the city, but then were forced to flee north and then east. The two forces never met.

Dahlgren and his troops ended up in King and Queen County, where they were attacked by home forces led by Captain James Pollard. The Confederates set a trap for the Yankees at what is today called Dahlgren's Corner near Stevensville and Mantapike. The

The tavern at King and Queen Courthouse was saved by the quick thinking of county residents.

Statues on the grounds of many Southern courthouses are reminders that the Civil War was not so long ago. This one stands in the courtyard at King and Queen Courthouse, a stone's throw from the tavern.

This statue is dedicated to the soldiers and sailors of King and Queen County who fought in the Civil War.

result of the battle was that Dahlgren was killed and several Union soldiers were captured.

When news came that Dahlgren had been shot to death in King and Queen County and that citizens of the county had helped in the attack, Kilpatrick sent over a thousand troops from Gloucester Point to the county on March 10. Their mission was to make the citizens pay for their part in the battle.

The federal troops burned the King and Queen County courthouse, the clerk's office, the jail, several stores, and a home in the village. The only building spared was the tavern. As Mrs. Gray related it, the Union forces went from building to building, burning "everything and anything." When the Yankees ordered everyone out of the tavern, several local people spoke up that a sick man was bedridden upstairs.

The Yankee captain ordered several men to go upstairs and get the man out of the house. Before going into the building, one of the soldiers asked, "What's wrong with him?"

A King and Queen County man in the crowd yelled, "He has smallpox!"

With that, the Yankees left the building and moved onto the next one. The tavern was spared and is today one of the finest buildings in the courthouse complex.

Legend has it that there was no one upstairs and that only the quick thinking of the citizens saved the building from the torch.

8

MARY'S WARNING

"When I was a boy, there were wooden crosses on many of these graves. The crosses were made from cedar and would last a long time. They're all gone now. The only thing left are sunken holes," said William Dickerson. He had purchased the land that held an old slave graveyard on Nesting Farm in Virginia. His ancestors are buried there—the same ones who passed this story down to him.

The screams and cries from inside the barn grew fainter and fainter as a crowd of slaves gathered outside the closed barn doors. Several white men with rifles stood guard in front of the door. A black woman knelt on the ground clutching the head of a man who lay there bleeding.

Mary, the slave woman on the ground, screamed, "You're killing my baby." Her husband, James, was the man on the ground, blood running from his mouth. One of the guards had belted him when he tried to push his way through to save their fourteen-year-old son, Jacob.

Jacob's cries grew faint but the sound of the whip slashing against his body never faltered. Mary began to cry, and James just hung his head and cried out in pain. "Don't kill my boy, Massa."

Suddenly, two men rode up and jumped off their horses. "Out of my way!" yelled the taller man as he ran into the barn.

The man was Russell Corbin, owner of Corbin Hall, among the largest farms in the county. Corbin was big and stocky and in his younger years had been a powerful man.

"Damn it, damn it," screamed Corbin, "you've killed another one!"

The door to the barn swung open, and Corbin dragged out a small, weaselly looking fellow from inside the barn. Corbin snatched the whip from the man's hand and struck him twice.

"Daddy, Daddy, don't hit me again," the man screamed.

Corbin threw the whip at him and fell to his knees. "Lord, may God forgive you," he said.

Mary ran into the barn, screaming, "Cut him down, James! Cut him down!"

When James walked through the door his wife was covered in the blood of their son. She was trying to stop him from swinging. The boy had been tied by his feet from the loft and was dangling upside down from the rope. James fell to his knees screaming and beating the ground. Jacob was dead.

"God, get a doctor," screamed John Copper, Corbin's slave overseer who had arrived with Corbin.

"There's no need for that," said Corbin with his head lowered. He got up off his knees and walked over to his son, Mutt, a short sickly fellow who all his life had tried in vain to meet the great expectations of his father. Corbin had been a military leader and a successful politician.

"I ought to let that man have you," said Corbin, speaking of James. "Go to the house and wait for me there," he said. "I've got to clean up this mess and then I'll deal with you."

Suddenly, Mary darted out of the barn with a pitchfork in her hands. She ran directly towards Mutt with the ten-tine pitchfork pointed at his heart. The two white men grabbed her, pulled the pitchfork from her hands, and pushed her to the ground.

She raised her head and spoke emphatically, "May your soul burn in hell and may God strike you from the face of the earth and banish your name from the minds of all men." She dropped her head and cried as she beat her fists on the ground.

"But Daddy, the little darky could count," said Mutt, as he ran to his horse. "You know they ain't suppose' to be able to count."

Corbin did not acknowledge Mutt, he was so astonished by the way the black woman had spoken. "Where did you learn to speak like that?" Corbin asked the woman.

"They came from old man Sibley's estate," answered the overseer Cop, as he was called by the slaves and others.

"Sibley's, over in New Kent County?"

"Yes sir, Mr. Corbin," replied Cop. "He taught them to read and write and how to speak properly."

"What have we got them doing?" asked Corbin.

"James is good with horses and we have him working in the barn," answered the overseer. "Mary works in your kitchen, sir. They've been here for three weeks."

"Cut the boy down and bury him in the graveyard at Salvo. I want these two moved to Salvo, too," said Corbin. "I don't want her working in my kitchen."

Corbin then got on his horse and turned to go. He paused and turned back, "Could he really count?" he asked Cop.

"Yes sir, as good as you and I," he replied, "and a lot better than Mutt. That's probably what got him going on this."

"This matter is closed! Everybody go home!" Corbin said, and he rode away.

Salvo was a small farm that Corbin owned in the next county far away from Mutt and Corbin Hall.

In those days, many slave owners would not allow their slaves to be educated for fear they would learn enough to want to run away to the North. During the Civil War, many slaves did run off to freedom by swimming or poling skiffs to Yankee ships that were coming and going on southern rivers.

Many plantation owners also felt education was only for the upper class. Most whites and slaves in tidewater Virginia were not offered the opportunity to go to school. The lack of any type of public education kept everyone in their place.

Most slave owners felt that the less their slaves knew the easier it would be to keep them "down on the farm." There were some, however, who made an attempt to educate their slaves. James, Mary, and Jacob's first master felt this way. Unfortunately, he had died and the slave family was sold off in the estate sale at which Corbin bought all of Sibley's slaves.

This wasn't the first time that Mutt had killed a slave. In fact, this was the third time it had happened. He suffered from an inferiority complex, and he would take his frustrations out on the slaves. From birth, he had been small and wormy-looking. He had a narrow pointed head and big ears that stuck out too far. His arms and legs were needle size and he spoke with a squeaky voice well into manhood. Unlike his brothers and sisters, who had made their way in the world with help from their wealthy father, Mutt was unable to succeed at anything.

He was an embarrassment to the Corbin household. But he was a Corbin, and God forbid any Corbin not look out for one of their own.

The killing of a slave by his master was not acceptable behavior, even in those times, but Mutt was a Corbin so the matter was closed as far as his family was concerned. James and Mary were moved to Salvo, and their son was buried in the slave graveyard on Salvo Farm.

Some years later, Mutt journeyed to Salvo to do some business for his father. On the way, he stopped at a country store not far from the farm. Some boys there were talking about rabbit hunting. Mutt was a good shot with a rifle, and the Corbins had some of the best rabbit dogs in the state.

The boys told Mutt about this place on Salvo Farm where their dogs would not hunt. They told him that they had never killed a rabbit in that area. Yet they had seen rabbits run there; somehow they would disappear before they could shoot them.

Mutt laughed at such talk and before he left made a bet with the boys that he would kill ten rabbits. Several weeks later Mutt came back with his best hunting dogs and, along with the boys, went out on the trail of some rabbits. He killed numerous rabbits but when they came to that place in the wood where no rabbits had been killed, Mutt's best dog would not run.

"What is this place?" asked Mutt. "Why is the ground all sunken in spots?"

"It's where the slaves from Salvo are buried," said one of the boys. "I don't like it in here. I'm going on back. If you bring out a rabbit, you win the bet."

Mutt hunted over the patch of ground for several hours, and towards the end of the day the boys heard a shot. "Well, I guess he got that rabbit," said one.

When Mutt came out he was carrying his prized dog. It was dead, with a bullet in its head. Mutt had an expression of fear in his eyes. He threw the dead dog on the back of his horse, mounted up, and said, "I'll be back."

Several days later, Mutt made the journey back to Salvo with another dog and this time went directly to the old slave graveyard site. It was towards the end of the day that a shot was fired and then several minutes later a second shot was heard.

When Mutt did not come back by dark, Cop and several slaves went out to the woods with lanterns, looking for him. They found Mutt sitting by a tree stump with his dog beside him. Both were dead, shot with Mutt's rifle.

The Corbins buried Mutt in the family graveyard at Nesting, a farm very near Corbin Hall. Russell Corbin did not want him buried in the main graveyard at Corbin Hall because he had been such a disgrace to the family.

His father had a large tombstone placed over Mutt's grave with his name and the dates of birth and death. Corbin had remembered the words of the slave woman when she screamed out that Mutt's name should be banished from the minds of men forever. He wanted all the slaves to see that Mary's threat had not come true.

Over the years, there were many stories and tales spread as to just what had happened to Mutt Corbin that day. One story was that some years later a young black boy and his dog were hunting at the graveyard site on Salvo Farm. Suddenly, a rabbit darted into a stump and the dog ran after him. When the rabbit came out, the boy aimed his gun. Like magic, the one rabbit broke in two, three rabbits right before his eyes. One ran to the left, the other to the right and another ran right for him. Startled by what he was seeing, the boy lowered his gun and didn't shoot. And there, standing right in front of him, was his dog. If he had shot, the dog would surely have been killed.

When the dog ran off after one of the rabbits, the boy turned to see where he was going, but when he turned back around, there was a black boy standing in front of him

"Don't you know that this is sacred ground to our people? Do not hunt here," said the boy to the young hunter.

The hunter called his dog and told the boy that he would leave. As he was going, he turned and glanced back over his shoulder to get a last look at the boy. He too was walking away and the hunter could see his bare back: he carried the scars of Mutt Corbin's whip.

Some speculate that Mutt also ran into this same boy and, when he saw who it was, took his own life.

Could it have been Jacob?

In 1987, William Dickerson of Pittsburgh, Pennsylvania, and I visited a slave graveyard that was on old Nesting Farm in Virginia. We walked across land that was covered in honeysuckle and towering pines as he recalled many of the stories that had been passed down from his relatives about the people who were buried here. One of those was the story of Mutt Corbin and the slave boy, Jacob.

Later, Mr. Dickerson and I walked across a field to see the great tombstones of the family that had owned all these slaves. Dickerson was a little ahead of me; suddenly he stopped and looked back at me in astonishment. Covered in vines was a grand fence that had obviously marked the site of a graveyard, but all the tombstones were gone, including the gravestone of Mutt Corbin.

9

CORNSTALK MUSKETS AND TA-TUM, TA-TUM, TA-TUM

Pat Perkinson of Topping, Virginia, lives in an old family home, Prospect, in Middlesex County. She shared several wonderful short stories with me in March 1998 that related to the war and her family.

Eubank Horse

When Kilpatrick's "mounted devils" came into Middlesex, word spread quickly throughout the county that Yankees were in the area. The Eubanks of Prospect had a favorite horse and knew the Yankees would take that horse if it was left in the barn.

The family story was passed down that slaves led the horse into the house, up the wide stairway, and into a room upstairs.

When the Yankees came to Prospect, near Grey's Point, they did not check to see what was in the upstairs rooms and left without taking the horse.

When the slaves went back to bring the horse down, it threw a fit and wouldn't allow them to touch it. The family decided to leave it there for a while for fear it might come through the ceiling. They figured that eventually it would get tired of being upstairs and

Pat and Bert Perkinson of Prospect shared several family tales of the Civil War.

come down gently. The horse, however, had a different notion and stayed in the room for several days with its head hanging out a window until finally it was led back down.

The stairway at Prospect still carries notches caused by the hooves of the Eubanks' favorite horse that climbed the stairs to escape the Yankees.

Prized Ladle

About the same time that Kilpatrick's "mounted devils" raided Prospect, they also raided Mrs. Perkinson's birthplace, Clifton, which is about fifteen miles from Prospect, near Warner, Virginia. Clifton was an early 1800s Dutch-roof–style home located in an area along the Dragon Run then known as the Forest.

Prospect, near Topping, Virginia, still has notches in the steps of its stairway where the family horse was led upstairs out of harm's way.

In 1849, Mrs. Perkinson's great-grandfather, James Augustus Blakey, purchased Clifton, and twelve years later the Civil War began. Kilpatrick's raiders came upon Clifton and ransacked it, taking whatever they could get in their saddlebags and pockets.

A Yankee took the family's prized silver ladle that had been in the Blakey family for generations. The Blakey "B" was engraved on the handle. A Yankee soldier stuck the ladle, handle down, in his hip pocket and galloped down the lane.

Before he could get out of sight of Clifton, the ladle fell from his pocket and his horse's hoof dented its bowl. Once the Yankees were gone, the Blakey family all came out to see what damage they had done. One of the family members found the ladle on the ground.

Mrs. Perkinson still has that dented ladle, and it is one of her most prized possessions.

Salt House Cove

During the Civil War, and perhaps before, the people of Prospect got their salt by collecting water from the Rappahannock River in wooden troughs and allowing it to evaporate. From what Charles Ferneyhough remembers was told him by his mother, Salome Stiff Ferneyhough, granddaughter of Major and Mrs. James Archer Eubank of Prospect, the method was as follows:

Large wooden traylike structures, ten feet wide, twenty feet long, and five or six inches high, were placed on several sawhorses on the creek bank adjacent to the old ferry landing. [There once was a ferry that came into Lockey's Creek from the Northern Neck, across the Rappahannock.] Salt water from the creek was poured into the trough. After the water disappeared by soaking into the wood and by evaporation, the salt was scraped off. It usually amounted to something less than a cupful, but it was the only salt folks had for table use and for curing hams, fish, and other meats.

Charles also remembers a family story about an enemy ship approaching after lookouts spied the strange saltbox apparatus on the shore. When it was determined that it was not part of a fortification, the ship went away.

Appomattox Sweetheart

Bert Perkinson, Mrs. Perkinson's husband, also had family connections to the Civil War. His maternal grandfather, Robert Terry Totty, served not only as an enlisted man in Lee's army, but also spent several months in the Confederate navy. The story of how Totty met his wife carries with it a touch of romance that will melt the heart.

Totty fought in numerous battles and faced death many times, but the saddest day of the war for him was April 10, 1865—the day he was paroled at Appomattox.

However, at the surrender, Totty saw a lovely young woman on horseback who was very much disturbed by the attention given her by a triumphant Yankee soldier. She was scolding the Yankee when Totty rode to the rescue. Even though he was on the losing side and Lee was surrendering his entire army to the Yankees, Totty cautioned the enemy soldier not to do something he would regret. The Yankee backed away and left the young lady alone.

On Christmas Day 1865, Totty, at twenty-five years of age, married his Appomattox sweetheart, Miss Mary Mildred Nowlin, whom he had met in April on horseback. The courtship had lasted just eight months before wedding bells rang.

Saving Wheatland

I first met Fielding Lewis Dickerson in 1992 at Wheatland, his ancestral home place on the Rappahannock River in Essex County. I was on assignment for the *Sentinel* and I took a tour boat from Tappahannock to the old Saunders steamboat wharf. Saunders wharf is one of the last original steamboat wharves on the Chesapeake. Wheatland was built in 1810 by John Saunders, Dickerson's great-grandfather. Fielding graciously shared this story with me.

"Legend has it that when the Yankees came upon Wheatland during the Civil War, a northern commander aboard a warship issued an order to burn it to the ground. The northern officer commanded

Robert Terry Totty fought for the South in both the army and navy. His grandson, Bert Perkinson, recalls the story of how Robert met his wife at Appomattox
on the last day of the war.

Fielding Lewis Dickerson recalled the story of how his great-grandfather saved his home place.

Saunders to get everyone out of the house. Instead, Saunders called everyone—slaves, children, and adults—to the house and ordered them to the front porch steps where the Yankees could see them clearly. Saunders then hollered, 'If you are going to take Wheatland, then you will have to take us all!' The Yankees then turned their guns on a nearby barn and blew it to pieces, leaving Wheatland and its stubborn owner safe and sound."

Saving Hewick

Charlie Palmer remembers his father, who fought alongside Captain Billy Christian of Urbanna, telling this story to him when he was a child. Charlie was born in 1889.

"From time to time, Captain Billy, as he was called by most who knew him, would come home from the war to check on his family,

Wheatland on the Rappahannock River was saved from the Yankees by its owner, John Saunders, who refused to leave when cannons from Yankee gunboats were aimed at his home.

some of whom lived at the colonial homesite Hewick, just outside Urbanna.

"Captain Billy had worked out a plan to keep the Yankees from coming around and stealing everything they could find. It was his opinion that most Yankees riding through the countryside in small groups were more likely to pass up a fight if they were not pressed into battle.

"His method was simple. There were many slaves living at Hewick, so Captain Billy had them cut cornstalks about the height of a rifle and he aligned the cornstalks so they looked like a circle of rifles—like when stacked in a camp. He instructed slaves to place the cornstalks in the barn at night and to have them out in the yard during the day as visible as possible from the road.

"He also instructed them to cut enough stalks for every man, woman, and child at Hewick to have one. Captain Billy drilled them on how to march with a stalk over their shoulder so that, from a distance, it just might look like a large number of Confederate soldiers.

"On one occasion when Captain Billy was home, a small group of mounted Yankee soldiers were spotted out on the road not far from Hewick. Captain Billy gathered everyone and had each one take a cornstalk. They marched back and forth in the yard.

"The road to Hewick was very long and from a distance the Yankees could see all the activity. Legend has it they rode away, preferring not to do battle on that day with the strong force of Confederates marching on the grounds of Hewick."

Yankees Killed a Rabbit

Another family story from Charlie was about the time Yankee gunboats bombarded Urbanna, which forced relatives and friends to hide behind the high banks on the creekside to try to escape enemy shells.

General George McClellan was commander of the Army of the Potomac from July 1861 to November 1862. Sometime in 1862 McClellan formulated a plan to take Richmond by attacking from the east. The plan was called the Urbanna plan because McClellan planned to spearhead the attack through Urbanna, a small town on the Rappahannock River that had an excellent deepwater harbor and was about sixty miles from Richmond.

Fortunately for Urbanna, McClellan was replaced in November 1862 before he could get his plan off the ground. However, prior to his departure, he sent several warships down to soften the town by bombardment and make things ready for an attack.

The ships anchored off the mouth of the creek and began firing cannonballs at the town. When the townsfolk heard the firing they all ran to the bottom of the high banks on the sides of Urbanna Creek.

Charlie recalls that an old man named Colonel John Montague stayed at the top of the bank with a spyglass and every time he saw the flash of fire from a cannon he would scream, "Squat!"

The colonial home of Hewick near Urbanna, Virginia, was saved from a Yankee attack by a group of family members and slaves marching with cornstalks on their shoulders.

Several cannonballs hit homes and buildings in Urbanna but the standing joke was that the only thing the Yankees killed that day was an old hare that didn't make it to its hole before the firing began.

Yankee/Reb Hideout

This story was shared with me by the late Hugh Norris of Deltaville, Virginia.

A widow lady who lived on Stingray Point in Deltaville had two sons. One of her sons fought for the North and the other for the

South. During the war, the boys would come home from time to time to see their mother. For fear of being captured, they made a hideout in some thick underbrush there on the place. The Yankee son was always fearful that he would be captured behind enemy lines and the Confederate son feared being captured by the Yankees that were forever present, it seemed, in areas of Virginia where there was not a great deal of fighting. The Yankees also had a large camp at Fishing Bay, just a few miles down the road.

When there was word that troops were in the neighborhood and both boys were home, they would both go to the hideout. Their mother had worked out a signal system: one ring of the dinner bell meant Confederate troops were in the area and two rings meant Yankee troops.

If Yankees were on the property, her Yankee son would come out of the wood to greet his comrades and encourage them not to take anything from his poor mother. He would also provide the troops with a list of other houses to search to get them away from his brother who was in the hideout.

When Confederates would come, their mother would ring the bell once and her rebel son would come out from hiding. He would also encourage his comrades to leave his poor mother alone and would offer suggestions to get them off the property in a hurry.

After the war, the two brothers moved back to Deltaville and lived on the property that had belonged to their mother. Their differences of opinion over the war were never an issue. "After all, they were brothers," said Captain Hugh.

The Ride Home

When I was a boy, Bill Ryland taught me in Sunday School at the Urbanna Baptist Church. He was my first boy scout leader. I spent hours at his home as a boy playing Ping-Pong on the back porch overlooking the Rappahannock River with his youngest son, Nugget.

I was asked by Fred Gaskins, publisher and editor of the *Southside Sentinel*, to go and talk to Mr. Ryland about his father, Walter H. Ryland. The assignment was a piece on the history of the *Sentinel*. The paper was celebrating its one hundredth anniversary. Walter Ryland had owned the paper from 1897 until his death in 1915.

During our conversation, Mr. Ryland shared with me this short story about his grandfather, the Reverend John W. Ryland, who was at Appomattox during the last days of the war.

"I don't remember too many stories about the war but I know my grandfather was badly wounded at the Battle of Seven Pines and his best friend was looking after him when the next thing you know his best friend was killed.

"At the end of the war, Grant was so good to give us all the broken-down horses and mules that were left over. The Yankees held a drawing for animals and my grandfather drew a white mule. Another friend from King and Queen County drew a horse, but the horse died before they left for home. So granddaddy and his friend rode and walked from Appomattox to Church View on that white mule.

"They would take turns—one would ride and the other would walk and they did this all the way home."

10

A NAME OF MY OWN

"During slave times, we got our names in different ways. Early on, we only had first names and then they gave us last names. Sometimes we were named for the families who enslaved us and sometimes it came from whoever decided to give us a name," recounted William Dickerson of Pittsburgh, Pennsylvania, whose grandmother was born a slave on Nesting Plantation near Jamaica, Virginia.

It was early spring of 1861 on the Custis farm on the Northern Neck of Virginia. The coal oil lamps had been burning all night in the farmhouse, and the sun was still several hours away from rising.

Sam Dover had stayed up the entire night. He was readying himself for a trip that he had made many times before as the slave overseer of the Custis farm, where he lived in a small, neatly kept house near a row of slave shanties.

A dry growing season had severely damaged the crops that year. To make up for lost income, Master Custis, owner of the farm, decided he would have to sell some of his slaves.

He was going to sell Black Will, his wife Birdie, and their three children, mostly because he felt they would fetch a big price and also because both adults were field hands. If either had worked in the Big House, Master Custis's wife and children would fret over losing their favorite slaves.

When Master Custis sold slaves, he tried to sell them as a family. He would tell people that his heart would not allow him to split families, but the truth was that he believed he could get more money for an entire family. Also, if family members were left behind, they would often create problems.

Children did not always bring a big price, but if the mother and father were strong and sturdy, the buyer would often pay a little more, thinking that the children might grow up to be big and strong too. Black Will and Birdie were strong and healthy.

There was yet another reason Master Custis had decided on Black Will: His back was smooth "as a stone rounded down by the sea." The first thing a slave buyer looked for was a scarred back. If there were scars, it meant that the slave was beaten regularly and more than likely was a troublemaker.

Sam Dover, the Custis overseer, had a reputation for beating slaves to keep them in line, and his reputation was widespread. When Mr. Street, a slave buyer from Water View, Virginia, came to inspect the family, he was impressed that Black Will's back was not scarred. He agreed to pay a premium price for the family.

On the day Mr. Street inspected the slaves, Sam Dover had showed him several other families too, because he did not want Black Will or the other slaves to know who was up for sale. If a slave thought he was going to be sold away from his family, he just might try and run off with them.

Ordinarily, Black Will was a good-natured fellow. He and Birdie had been born on the Custis farm and always seemed content living there. Sam, however, wasn't going to take a chance on losing a sale or perhaps losing a valuable piece of property, so Black Will would have to be put in irons.

Before light, Sam and a group of hired hands went to the Big House to get last-minute instructions from Master Custis, who told them that he did not want Black Will to be cut or bruised. "If he puts up a fight, don't hurt him bad," said Master Custis. "Before you put shackles on him, make sure you wrap burlap strips around his ankles and wrists." The burlap would keep the shackles from bruising his skin. He did not want the buyer to know that the slave had to be chained to make the trip.

In the dark, the white men went to Black Will's shanty. They lined up on each side of the shanty door and Sam yelled in as he did every morning before light, "All right, Black Will, let's get to work! Those old milk cows need some relief."

One of Black Will's jobs was to milk the cows that supplied cream, milk, and butter to those living on the farm—black and white.

"I'se comin, Massa Sam," said Will.

When he opened the door, the men jumped him. Black Will didn't put up much of a fight until he realized what was happening and then he screamed, "Oh sweet Jesus, Massa, don't take my family away from me. Please, Massa! I love Birdie and my children."

"We ain't, Black Will," said Sam. "Your family is going with ya."

"Don't lie to me, Massa Sam," Will screamed as the men pushed him face down on the ground and chained his hands behind him and put the shackles on his legs.

The rest of the slaves could hear the commotion but not a door opened. They knew what was happening because they had heard those screams before. They knew that before the sun was up and the day had begun, someone would be gone.

"All right, Birdie, get on out here with your young'uns," yelled Sam, who had lost his hat in the commotion.

"Damn it, Black Will, you've dirtied up my hat," he said, picking it up and hitting Will in the head with it.

"I'se sorry, Massa Sam," said Will.

Birdie and the children were dragged into a wagon with only the clothes on their backs.

Four of the men jumped on their horses, while one took the reins of the wagon and another jumped in the back with shotgun in hand. The group stopped to meet Master Custis at the Big House. He would ride his favorite white stallion, Senator, on the trip. Food had been packed for all and was put in the bottom of the wagon—the trip would probably take a day and a half. They were meeting Mr. Street at a spot not far from his farm near Water View.

There was fear and misunderstanding in the eyes of the children, and Birdie tried her best to comfort them. She told them that at least the family was together and because of that they were luckier than most. She was, however, as scared as the children. She wondered where they were going and what kind of place their new home would be. She was also afraid that they might be going to the auction block and that the family would be split up forever.

She tried to comfort Black Will, who lay motionless in the bottom of the wagon, while a shotgun remained pointed at his head.

The trip required crossing the Rappahannock River by ferry and winding through Essex County down into Middlesex County toward old Street's farm.

Mr. Street had bought slaves from Master Custis before and he preferred to meet away from his farmhouse. If there were problems during the transfer, he didn't want his slaves to see the commotion. Not far from where they were to meet, Sam ordered the group to stop. Black Will was released from his chains and Sam told him that if he made any kind of commotion, one of his children would be shot on the spot. "Black Will, I ain't going to kill you and you know it, but I'll blast one of them little ones away," Sam threatened. When they got to the spot, Mr. Street and a group of white men were waiting. Most were neighbors of Street; they helped one another when these times came.

"How ya do there, Mr. Custis?" said Mr. Street. "I see ya brought my slaves. I hope they're in good shape after the trip."

"There were no problems at all, Mr. Street," said Master Custis. Mr. Street inspected each slave and then the two men went to the other side of the road to finish their business. Mr. Street paid in gold coins, which was the deal the two men had struck.

"Now, Mr. Custis, what names do these slaves have?" asked Mr. Street loud enough for all across the road to hear.

He told him their names.

"What is their last name, sir?"

"They don't have a last name. I'll leave that up to you, Mr. Street."

"Well, sir, since they have come from your place, can I name them Custis after you?"

"Dear God in heaven, don't do that, sir. I've never been with a black wench to have had a half-black bastard."

There were big fields on both sides of the road where the two men were standing. Mr. Custis pointed to the fields around them. "Why don't you call them Fields?"

"Good idea, sir. I will do that."

Black Will and Birdie were freed after the war but lived out their days just down the road from Mr. Street's farm. One of their children, Robert Fields, who was in the wagon that day in 1861, told this story to his granddaughter, Teresa Fields Bryant. She was born in the Jamaica District of Middlesex County on May 21, 1901.

One time when she was small her grandfather took her alone for a ride down a country road in a horse-drawn wagon. When he came to a certain spot, he pulled the wagon over to the side of the road between two big fields and, with tears in his eyes, retold the story of how he got his last name. Mrs. Bryant lives in Philadelphia now, but there are still several families of Fields who live in the Water View, Virginia, area. All are related to Black Will and Birdie.

11

MRS. KELLY'S COW

Many people living in the South did not take up the Confederate cause. One such man was William Henry Kelly. In 1858, Kelly, of Baltimore, Maryland, purchased a 133-acre farm in what was to become Deltaville, Virginia, at the tip of the Middle Peninsula. Tired of city living, he moved his family there in hopes of starting a new life.

When the war broke out, Kelly was not sympathetic to the southern cause and enlisted in the Union army. His wife Nancy and their children continued to live in Virginia behind Confederate lines. Although William was a Union soldier this did not keep Nancy from having to deal with the Yankee occupation of tidewater Virginia. The Yanks believed that anyone living in Virginia was the enemy and they treated them as such—that is, until they ran into Mrs. Kelly.

I am grateful to the late Hugh Norris who shared this story with me over fifteen years ago. I remember quite vividly the day we talked. It was a hot summer day, but we sat comfortably in his front porch swing catching a cool breeze off Jackson Creek. He was reminiscing about things that were told to him by old people when he was a child. This was the story he related to me as I remember it.

The war took its toll on families living in the South whether they were sympathetic to the North or the South. Nancy Kelly and her children were living between two enemies. Nancy's husband was a Yankee soldier, which did not sit well in the southern community where she was living. Most folks in rural tidewater Virginia were ardent southern sympathizers.

Nancy also had to deal with Yankees who came to the area. When they came, the Yanks did not ask about political beliefs. They took for granted that if you lived in the South, you were mothers, sisters, and children of Johnny Rebs.

The Yankees came on a regular basis to Middlesex County, Virginia, in an effort to capture Confederate soldiers either home on leave or home for health reasons. There was also considerable activity supportive of the Confederate cause going on up and down the rivers between the Northern Neck and the Middle Peninsula and the Yanks were trying to discourage these operations.

Union forces would sail down the Chesapeake Bay from Point Lookout, Maryland, and set up camp at Fishing Bay, about two miles from the Kelly home place. It is a good bet that William Kelly felt fairly secure that his family would not be harassed by the men

The home of Nancy and William Kelly still stands in Deltaville today where it is known as the "Kelly House."

who were fighting in the very same army that he was. Nancy's first encounter with Union troops, however, did not go well.

The first time Yankee troops arrived in the Deltaville community, they went from house to house taking what they could find to eat and anything else of value. When they came to Mrs. Kelly's house they didn't know that William was fighting in the Union Army. They killed the family's chickens and then tied a rope to the family cow and walked it to the Yankee camp to provide milk for the troops.

Nancy was beside herself. Here she was with a family to feed and a husband who was off fighting a war on the side of the very men who had killed her chickens and taken her cow.

She was livid and pumped up with courage. She got a neighbor to stay with her children and proceeded to walk to Fishing Bay to get her cow back. When she arrived, she demanded to see the officer in charge. She bristled as she told him that she wanted her cow back "right now!" She told the officer that her husband fought on the same side as he, that she had small children at home to feed, and that she needed her cow for milk to survive the hard times.

The officer was taken aback by this woman's courage and very quickly apologized. He ordered his men to return Mrs. Kelly's cow, and he also gave her several prize laying hens that had been taken from her neighbors. The officer then commanded several men to escort Mrs. Kelly home. Some carried the chickens in coops, while one soldier drove the cow home and another walked alongside as a guard.

The community watched as Nancy was escorted home with her cow and her neighbors' chickens. When the soldiers were gone, Nancy called to her neighbors to come and get their prize hens.

The neighbors were smart. "Why should we take them back? They'll just take them from us when they come back again. Why don't you keep them and we'll share the eggs?" Nancy agreed. The chickens stayed in her henhouse throughout the war. She and others in the community shared eggs, milk, and whatever else they had to keep the community from starving.

Captain Hugh Norris was born in 1899. This story was told to him by a relative—one of those neighbors of Nancy Kelly with whom she shared eggs and milk on a regular basis.

Nancy Kelly lived to the ripe old age of ninety-eight. She died in 1927 a beloved member of the Deltaville community.

12

A SLEEPING HOG

"During slave times, we were promised things, like food, but when it didn't come, many of us had to take to stealing. It was life or death for many of us. . . ." Clemon Brown's grandmother was a slave. She shared this story with Clemon's mother, who shared it with him.

It was unusually warm for a January day—one of those days in winter when the weather makes you think spring is right around the corner, but in reality old man winter has plenty of time left.

On this particular day, a crow soared and swooped in the sky as a blue jay chased its tail. The big black crow turned on the jay, but the smaller bird zigged and zagged to escape the clutches of the much bigger crow.

"Yes sir, old jay can get the best of big old crow 'most anytime," thought Moe Burgess, watching the chase. Moe was sitting on the front step of his shanty, enjoying the warmth of the day. His home was a flat-roofed shack that had once been a corncrib. There was only one small window towards the back to let light in and the big door on the front looked like a smokehouse door. Inside, there was a fireplace for cooking and to heat the shanty, a table and a few chairs, and a small rope bed that held a mattress filled with corn shucks. The shanty was clean and well kept.

Moe was a free Negro. His mother was a white woman, and Virginia law allowed any child of a white woman to be free. Moe's wife Mabel had been a slave, but he had bought her freedom from old man Curtis. Moe had earned his living as a blacksmith; he paid for his wife's freedom with gold coins.

Moe had worked hard; he was old now and looked it. He had lost a portion of his foot back in the 1850s when a mule stepped on it and broke it into many pieces. He had been hobbling around for years. Sometimes he used a crutch he had made from the forked branch of a hickory tree and sometimes he used a twisted walnut cane. Moe had found a small walnut tree in the woods where a wild grapevine had grown around the slender trunk. When he pulled the vine away, the bark had come off the stick and left a twisted impression on the wood. It was a most unusual cane, admired by many. Moe was proud of his cane and he used it whenever he went to the store on Saturday night or to church on Sunday. He was also particularly pleased that several white folks in the community had from time to time tried to buy his special cane.

As Moe watched the birds, he had his cane leaning against the step beside him. There was a broom straw in his mouth and a wool hat on his head. Mabel had gone down the road to Callis' store to fetch some coal oil. She needed it to fuel the lamps inside the shanty and also to mix up some medicine for her chickens that had lice. She had an old home remedy where she would mix coal oil with lard and rub it on and under the feathers of her birds. It would get rid of the lice every time.

Neither Moe nor Mabel knew exactly how old they were, but they had lived on that little slice of land on the outskirts of the Curtis plantation for over sixty years. Moe had been tolerated over the decades by white and black alike because of his skill as a blacksmith, but many thought he was a little touched in the head and he liked it that way.

At that time, whites and some blacks would attend church together. Moe, Mabel, and all the other blacks worshipped from the balcony. Sometimes on Sunday Moe would just start talking about anything right in the middle of the service and it would embarrass Mabel to death, even though it was all perfectly harmless.

With the blue jay safely away, Moe gave a rousing yell as if to cheer on the bird for having safely pecked the crow and escaped to fight another day. He raised his cane high and yelled, "That'll teach you to mess with old jay."

About the time the jay and the crow finished their show, a black man driving a wagon and two young black boys on horseback rode up to Moe's shanty. The man pulled the wagon over to the side of the lane and ran up to Moe.

"Ya got to help us, Moe," said the man. It was Hap Schools and his two sons. They were slaves on the Curtis farm.

"What's the matter, boys?" Moe asked.

Hap told Moe how Master Curtis had promised that his family would have ham and pork for the winter, but when it came time for sharing, Master Curtis said there wasn't enough to go around. "He said the Yankees took all his meat. Hell, his smokehouse is full of hams," said Hap angrily. "We've nearly starved all winter. I've eaten so much muskrat I've just about turned into one," said Hap in disgust.

"It sounds like Master Curtis is up to his old tricks," said Moe.

Suddenly, there was the loud sound of horses coming down the road. "Quick, boys, pull that hog out of the wagon. Take him inside and put him in my bed. Pull the covers up to his neck," said Moe.

They grabbed the hog and carried it inside the house. Moe hobbled in behind them. Once it was properly positioned in the bed, Moe turned the hog's head so that it would be facing away from the door and put one of Mabel's Sunday hats on its head. The hog had been gutted and had obviously been hanging in the smokehouse for some time. It was white as a ghost.

Just as they got finished inside the shanty, Master Curtis and his boys rode up to Moe's house. When they came close, Moe stepped outside and began to moan as if in great pain. The boys came out looking startled because they thought something was really wrong with Moe.

"All right, Hap, where the hell is my hog?" Master Curtis yelled and jumped down from his horse with pistol drawn.

"Hap and the boys have been here all morning, Master Curtis," said Moe, still moaning. "They came as soon as they heard."

"Heard what?" asked Master Curtis.

"Why—my Mabel! She's done died and gone to heaven."

"What killed her, Moe?" Master Curtis asked.

"She done died of diphtheria," said Moe.

When he mentioned diphtheria, the white men all took a step back. "I ain't heard nothing about Mabel being sick," said Master Curtis. "You're just trying to protect these no-counts. They stole my hog."

"It's so good of you to come to my little house and pay your last respects to my beloved Mabel," rambled Moe. "Go right on in and pay your last respects to her."

Master Curtis took a step toward the door and peered into the room. There was not much light in the small shanty, but he could see the white shape of what he thought was Mable. "My God, she's as white as a ghost," he said. "How long has she been dead?"

"Oh, about two weeks," said Moe. "Don't she look natural?"

"Two weeks! God's sake! Everything from here to town is probably contaminated," said Master Curtis.

"She's getting a little soft and beginning to smell a little bit," said Moe. "Is that what she's suppose' to do?"

"My God! Hap, help him get her in the ground. Let's get the hell out of here!" Master Curtis said.

They jumped on their horses and rode away. When they were a good distance away, Moe began to laugh, and the boys began to laugh too.

"Now, boys, I want me a good ham out of all this," said Moe. Hap promised him that he would bring him a ham. They put the hog in the back of the wagon and went on down the road.

When Mabel got home and Moe told her the story, she didn't think it was funny and asked what he was going to tell people when they saw her in church on Sunday.

"Ah, just tell them you were sick and your crazy husband thought you were dead," said Moe. "Them white folks think I'm half crazy anyway."

Several days later, Moe was outside watching his blue jay when Hap delivered a fresh ham to his house and thanked him again for his help.

13

YANKEE HOLE

In 1937, Mrs. Josie Henley Ellyson wrote down her recollections of life during the Civil War at the family farm of Hillsborough in King and Queen County, Virginia. Mrs. Ellyson tells a clear and vivid story of what happened when Yankees came to her family's doorstep and there was no one to protect them.

Mrs. Ellyson was born October 15, 1852, at Hillsborough. She was eighty-five when she wrote this piece for the King and Queen Chapter of the Virginia Women's Club. She lived to be ninety-six years old. Her memories have since become a family treasure.

I would like to thank William Todd Henley, Jr., and his family, who kindly agreed to allow me to use his aunt's recollections.

I was eight years of age when the War Between the States began in 1861. The events connected with it which happened in the neighborhood at my home Hillsborough, where I was born, are very vivid in my mind.

There was wild confusion and commotion throughout the country, especially among the men. As soon as war was declared they began daily to assemble at Bruington to be drilled in military tactics from anyone who had military training in such affairs, usually some ex-student from Virginia Military Institute. The young ladies from the countryside were always on hand to watch and maybe pray.

As the war progressed we could sit on the hillside at Hillsborough overlooking the Mattaponi River and could hear clearly the roar of cannons and firing of the big guns in the fighting around Richmond. [Richmond is about 45 miles from Hillsborough.] We would wonder all the while which of our relations and friends were giving their lives for the cause.

I had two uncles who held commissions: Lieutenant Atwood Walker, my mother's brother, and Captain Alexander Fleet Bagby, who had married my mother's sister, Fanny Walker. In April 1864, [Philip Henry] Sheridan's army tried to reach some gunboats on the York River. So they passed through King and Queen County. We heard that they were coming so we sat up all night preparing for their arrival. My father and brothers filled a wagon with provisions and took it and the horses down to the low ground where they

Built around 1740, Hillsborough was invaded by Philip Henry Sheridan's army during the Civil War. Josie Henley Ellyson was a girl at the time and recalls the way it was when the Yankees invaded her family home. Photo courtesy of Mary Steed Ewell.

thought it would be safely hidden and they went and hid. The Yankees would surely kill the men and boys.

The servants put the flat silver in an ice cream freezer, placed it in a barrel, and filled the barrel with ashes. Later someone thought this was an unsafe place and moved the freezer elsewhere. Sure enough, when the Yankees came they eyed the ash barrel with suspicion—turned it topsy turvy—but the flat silver escaped.

While we were at breakfast the next morning, we were surprised to hear the corn sheller in the granary going. We discovered that the Yankees had come through the low ground and had stopped at the granary to get corn to feed their horses. Over three hundred horses were tied to the locust trees in the yard and fed there. You can imagine how the yard at Hillsborough looked.

Family memorabilia left from the war hang on the walls of Hillsborough.

Then the Yankees began to plunder. They used their sabers to cut off our hens' heads, then they would tie the dead chickens to their saddles to take back to camp. My little brother, Todd, had a pet hen named Patty and when they called the fowl, she, of course, was the first one to lose her head.

Then the Yankees asked Nannie, the seamstress [a slave], where the meat was hidden since it was missing from the smokehouse. She replied that she did not know. They told her that they had rags soaked in oil and if they were not given the meat, the house would soon be in ashes.

So my mother told them it was in the attic. One of the Yankees found the little secret staircase in a closet to get up to the attic. When stepping from one rafter to another, one of them missed his step and put his foot through the ceiling. This hole has never been repaired and is a visible reminder of those dreadful days.

The Yankees went to the kitchen out in the yard and made a servant cook for them all day, using up all the food on hand and pouring out on the ground—flour, lard, preserves, pickles, meal, and everything—what they could not take with them.

One of them took my mother's breast pin from the pincushion on her bureau in her bedroom. Our Nannie [house slave] jerked it from his hand and said, "You shan't have Miss Betty's pin." The Yankee did not try to take it from her. I have this pin in my possession now.

Several of the Yankees tried to rob the beehive, but they had to retreat in defeat, much to the delight of us children. My mother always had a bench for flowers under a window that is now the dining room on which she had a Jerusalem cherry in bloom. We were taught that these cherries were poison. We watched with great glee as the Yankees ate the cherries, hoping the poison would work as we had been led to believe.

They also went into our parlor and played our piano, but much to our relief they did not destroy it as they had done in other homes.

A young colt broke its halter down in the low grounds where he had been hidden with the other horses and arrived at the house exactly at the wrong time. He was carried off, along with the mare that had a young colt across the road. This left the colt with no mother. When the Yankees could procure good horses, they would leave their old broken-down ones behind, which furnished the only means farmers had of cultivating their farms. The Yankees would brand 'U.S.' with a hot iron on the horses' shoulders.

When the Yankees left, there was not one mouthful of food left on the place for my mother, seven small children, and the servants to eat. We still had those provisions that we had hidden, but my father was afraid to bring them up for fear the Yankees would return.

Yankees emptied the smokehouse at Hillsborough.

Although the ceiling has been repaired over the years, the family has left "the Yankee hole" as a reminder that the war came to Hillsborough. A Yankee stuck his foot through the ceiling while searching for hams in the attic.

William Todd Henley, Jr., has heard the war stories many times from his aunts and other relatives who lived at Hillsborough during the war. Today he is the patriarch of Hillsborough.

Even in those days, as now, bad news travels fast. Our friends, the Littlepage [family] across the river heard of our plight and what joy we experienced when we saw a boat crossing the river with food aplenty for us hungry children.

Many of our soldiers were ill at Gloucester Point and, since there were no hospitals, they were distributed among the homes for their period of convalescence. Two were sent to Hillsborough: Jerry Flood and a Mr. Mosby, both from North Carolina. They both had clear ways of expressing themselves, especially Mr. Flood. Father loved to talk to him and derived great pleasure from his original expressions. He said the women of Raleigh "flung them blossoms" when they marched away and always called my Aunt Fanny Bagby "the fair one."

Later on, federal gunboats came up the [Mattaponi] river and shelled our home while we found refuge in the basement. On one occasion, Nannie was standing by the window with one of the young children, Aunt Betty, in her arms when a bullet whizzed past her head and buried itself in the door just back of her. This bullet was found last year when some repairs were being made. [It's] one more memento of that dreadful four-year conflict.

The gunboats proceeded up the Mattaponi River to Walkerton where the music lured many slaves away. [At night crewmen entertained themselves by playing music.] Quite a number of slaves working in the fields at Locust Grove just walked away in their shirt sleeves and boarded the boats, never more to see their homeland.

One of those who walked away was the husband of our faithful Nannie—how distressed she was! After the war was over, she followed him to Yorktown and there they opened a restaurant. When we went to the Centennial [of the ratification of the Articles of Confederation] in 1881, she served us fried oysters.

Cousin Suzy Davies and her four children from Gloucester County were refugees at Hillsborough. One evening we saw her husband riding down the road on a fine horse; he was on furlough from his command. The next morning his fine horse had died. We supposed food had been so scarce in the army that a normal feeding had killed it.

It was joyous news when we heard that the fearful four-year conflict was at an end. The changes in everything [that came at the end of the war] were very hard on my father. He died in October 1870, leaving my mother with a farm and seven children to raise. My oldest sister had married Melville Walker and lived at Locust Grove. We took as our motto: "Leave thou fatherless children. I will preserve them alive and let thou widows trust in me."

The Lord has been good to us. All but one lived to over three-score years and ten. The exception was my oldest brother Bernard who passed away at sixty-five from injuries received when his home burned. There are now remaining two over fourscore years. May we have faith in God's promises and believe He means what He says in His holy word."

14

CROSSING THE RIVER

For fifty years, the plain, round-top trunk lay hidden in a corner of the attic in the little two-room log house at King's Neck in Middlesex County, Virginia. It belonged to Louisa Walker, who had stored the Walker family treasures inside it many years before.

Inside that trunk was a Bible that dated back to 1875 with family names listed in it; dresses made from cloth flour and sugar bags that had been worn by Louisa when she was a slave on the Muse Farm near Towles Point in Lancaster County, Virginia; and a pair of store-bought ankle-high shoes that had the name William Walker roughly stitched on a piece of cloth sewn onto the tongue of one of the shoes.

The year was 1863. Dawn was still several hours away. William Walker and the other slaves were still asleep in bed. William's job as a slave was to mind the three cows that the Muse family kept in the barn out back. The cows supplied the household with milk and butter.

When the rooster crowed, William arose from his corn shuck mattress and climbed out from under his only blanket. The blanket was special to him because his mother had made it from scraps of cloth that she found left on the floor of the big house. He then ran across the dew-soaked yard from the one-room shanty to the barn. His feet were bare because Master Muse did not allow his slaves to wear shoes, even in the winter.

"It's a lot easier for a darky to run off with shoes on his feet," he would say to neighboring slave owners, who often encouraged him to look after his property better.

When William reached the barn, John Collins, the Muses' slave overseer, was already up and about. "Well, Billy boy, you won't be here much longer," said John.

William ran into the first stall and jumped right down next to Maggie, the best milk cow on the place. As the cow lay in the straw, William pushed his feet up under her to get them warm.

"I'm going to hate to see you go, boy. You're the only one who can do anything with these cows," said John, who worked right alongside the slaves. He was called an overseer but he had more compassion than most overseers in those days.

"I don't want to go, Master John," said William. "But Master Muse says we got to go with Missy Anne."

Anne Muse had just recently gotten married to a gentleman in Middlesex County and part of her dowry included William, his mother Eliza, and her three sisters, twins Mary and Martha and Marie Louisa. They were supposed to cross the river from Lancaster to Middlesex later that day on a raft. They were to carry furniture and other items that were part of Missy Anne's dowry.

Once William's feet were toasty warm, he pulled them out from under the cow and laid on his back and pushed against Maggie's side with both feet. "Get up, cow, it's time to give us milk," said William. He milked the three cows, cleaned the stalls, and, when he finished, paused to reflect on what had been his home his entire life.

There was the hayloft where he had played hide-and-seek when he was smaller and the stall where he first learned to milk a cow. On his first try, the cow kicked the milk bucket over, which tipped the stool over, and William went face-down into a big pile of cow dung.

With reluctance, the boy bade good-bye to the barn where he had so often retreated for security when there was trouble. There was the time old Turkey Head, a large black man who had been born on the farm, learned that Master Muse had sold him to a plantation down in Georgia. He started fussing and fighting and Master Muse had to call in some white folks from around and about.

Turkey Head could throw a punch, and he hit Master Muse so hard that they didn't think he'd ever get up off the ground. When the white men came from the other plantation, they threw Turkey Head down on the ground and put his hand on the chicken-killing block. One of the men raised an ax high over his head and threatened to cut his hand off if he did not calm down. Turkey Head begged the men not to cut his hand off and promised never to hit a white man again. Master Muse said to him, "We weren't going to cut it off anyway, Turkey Head, because what good would a slave be with only one hand? Besides, I'm going to send you down south and I told them you had two good hands and two good feet, but I suspect they're going to cut off one of your feet just to make sure you don't run off." Muse then gave a hearty laugh, and Turkey Head was put in shackles. The day it happened, William's mother had sent him to the loft and told him not to come down for any reason until all the screaming had stopped.

"What are you daydreaming about, boy?" asked Collins.

"Oh, just thinking about all the cow dung I've had to shovel out this barn. I bet it would fill up Master Muse's house," said William with a chuckle.

"Yeah, boy, I reckon it would just about fill it up," said Collins with a smile on his face.

Collins left and went up to the big house while William lingered a bit longer. He climbed the ladder to the loft and crawled across the hay to a corner where he had often gone just to think. It was his special place where his thoughts and dreams were all his own.

"I'm going to miss you, special place," he said to the corner. He placed his hand on a wood rafter and began to cry.

Suddenly the barn door opened, and William heard his mother's voice calling to him. "It's time, William," said his mother. "We've got to go across the river."

The day before, William had helped load some of the furniture on the barge, and he and Collins were to take the first load over. It

Sherman Holmes is the grandson of William Walker. The story of crossing the Rappahannock was one of his family's stories passed down from slave days. The late John Segar, an ancestor of William Walker's master, also contributed to this story.

was going to take several trips to get the slaves and all the furniture across.

"I'm coming Mamma," he said.

William wondered what it was going to be like across the river. He had heard that his new master's father had bought his son and new bride an old run-down farm on the Piankatank River and all the slaves were going to have to work hard to get it in shape for Missy Anne. Master and Missy Anne were going to live at Rosegill Farm across the creek from the town of Urbanna until their home was ready.

William had heard of the war that was going on to free the slaves and wondered what it might mean to him some day. But he did not think about it much.

The group had to walk down a steep hill and into a marsh to get to Muse's Landing on the Rappahannock. The marsh had a road cut through it with logs laid down and tied together with rope. The logs were set crossways, and flat planks were put down over the logs to make it sturdy. It was a decent road but a rough ride for those in horse and wagon. At the outer edge of the marsh was Muse's Landing.

The morning air over the river was heavy with fog, and Collins decided it was best to wait for the fog to burn off before making the trip. The slaves waited on the wharf for several hours. All their belongings were in a round-top trunk that Master Muse had given William's mother.

There was a silence in the air and over the water that was only disturbed by an occasional cricket chirping or the call of a great blue heron. Although it was spring, the air was still cool and the water temperature cold. The small group sat quietly on the shore, waiting. Along with William, his mother, and Collins were his mother's sisters, Mary, Martha, and Marie Louisa.

Suddenly, the quiet was broken as the group heard a horse and wagon bumping across the wooden road. "Now, who could that be?" said Collins to the slaves.

"Collins! Collins!" yelled a man from off in the distance. The slaves recognized the voice of Master Muse. "Don't leave yet!"

Master Muse and Missy Anne rode up to the landing in a buggy. "Collins, I want you to take Missy Anne with you."

"But we don't have enough room," said Collins.

"Nonsense," said Muse. "That barge can hold one more."

"I thought Missy Anne had gone over on the *Blackbird*," said Collins. The *Blackbird* was a schooner that hauled goods to and from the Muse plantation.

"She did, but she came back over yesterday and we had planned to let her ride the *Blackbird* back over today. But Captain Haynie sailed early this morning to the Potomac to pick up a load of lumber," said Master Muse.

"I don't like this," said Collins. "I'm not sure that we can get across with all these slaves, much less with your daughter and six trunks." The wagon was loaded down with trunks full of things belonging to Missy Anne.

Muse walked over to Collins and pulled him aside. "Come on, Collins. If you're worried about it, leave three of those women slaves here. They can go over later."

"I really don't like it, but I guess I don't have much choice," said Collins. "If you take Mary, Martha, and Marie Louisa back to the farm, I'll take Missy Anne and her trunks in their place."

"That will be just fine," said Muse.

"Hi, Missy Anne," said William, as he helped Collins stack the trunks on the barge.

"Hi, William. I'm so glad you and Eliza are going to be with me at Rosegill," she said.

They all sat for a little longer on the dock, and then the fog lifted.

"All right, William, let's get on across the river," said Collins. Collins and William had long poles that they used to shove off from the dock and out into the river as far as they could and still reach the bottom. Once underway, a sail was raised and the barge moved slowly toward the river channel. Collins was at the stern holding onto the steering pole when the wind began to gust.

"What's going on here?" Collins asked.

"I don't know," said William.

The wind slowed and, as if from nowhere, it began to rain. The raindrops were as big as quarters. Missy Anne, William, and Eliza crawled up under a canvas that was aboard to keep the furniture dry.

"Where the hell did this storm come from?" yelled Collins. Then suddenly a gust of wind hit with great force. The barge tipped to one side and the trunks slipped over the side and Anne and Eliza went overboard.

"For God's sake, hold on!" screamed Collins.

The only thing that kept William from going over was that he grabbed hold of the leg of a large dresser and held on tight.

"Mamma!" he screamed.

Eliza was holding onto one of Missy Anne's trunks that had gone overboard, but where was Missy Anne?

"Where is Anne?" screamed Collins.

William ran to each side of the barge looking for Anne. He saw his mother holding onto the trunk, but he could not see Anne.

Rosegill Plantation on the south side of the Rappahannock was the place where Missy Anne and her small band of slaves stayed while their new home was being refurbished on the Piankatank River.

"Help me!" came a scream that sounded very close to the barge.

"Where is she?" screamed Collins again.

Suddenly, William saw Anne's bonnet bobbing up and down as she fought to get to the surface.

William quickly grabbed a rope that was tied to the boom, wrapped it around his waist, and jumped in. When he got to Missy Anne she grabbed his arm and pulled him under.

William had to fight to get apart from her. When he did get loose, he reached out to her with his foot. She grabbed his bare foot and Collins pulled William and Anne to the boat.

They were both exhausted. They lay on the deck of the barge while Collins threw a rope to Eliza and rescued her.

Although some of Missy Anne's furniture and clothes were lost, she made it safely to Rosegill where her concerned husband was waiting on the shore.

Out of appreciation for saving his wife, their master assured William and Eliza that they would be house servants for the rest of their lives. Missy Anne had shoes made for every member of the family.

Eliza, Mary, Martha, and Marie Louisa discarded their slave shoes when freedom came but William placed his in the round-top trunk as a reminder of that day he crossed the Rappahannock and of his life as a slave on Muse Farm.

15

SAVING THE RECORDS

Philemon T. Woodward was clerk of the Middlesex County, Virginia, courts from 1852 to 1892. During the war he was ordered by the Confederate government to send county records that dated back to the 1600s to Richmond for safekeeping. The reason for this order was that whenever Yankee patrols or cavalry units would come upon an unguarded courthouse, they would burn and pillage whatever they could find—part of war is to destroy the spirit of one's opponents. Southerners took great pride in their heritage, and Yankees knew the destruction of longtime records would demoralize the South.

Woodward, however, had a different idea. He felt his records were safer elsewhere than in Richmond, where great battles would soon be fought. Accounts of how Philemon T. Woodward saved the county records have been told over and over again. There have been numerous versions of the story passed down from ancestors of whites and slaves who helped Woodward hide the boxloads of records. Supposedly, he never told where he hid the records, and it has been somewhat of a mystery to this day.

Perhaps a close-to-accurate story has come to light from the records of the late Walter Ryland, former owner and editor of the *Southside Sentinel*, the Middlesex County weekly newspaper. Ryland was editor and owner of the paper from 1898 until 1915. Sometime within those years, an article entitled "Historical Sketch Concerning Middlesex and the Town of Urbanna" was published in Ryland's newspaper:

"Generally during the war, the records of tidewater Virginia counties were burned in the great fire at the evacuation of Richmond.

"P. T. Woodward, one of the best clerks among the great clerks of Virginia, suggested to circuit court Judge Joseph Christian that Richmond would be the most unsafe place in the world to send our records. He told the judge that it would be the center of great contending armies and liable to be destroyed by fire at any time during the war, and certainly before it ended. He said if he received authority from Judge Christian he could conceal the records in a place where the Yankees would never find them.

"The judge gave him that authority. So Woodward boxed up all his deed books and court records and took them to the residence of an old gentleman who lived on an island in the Dragon Swamp [also known as Dragon Run] and deposited these boxes in his barn and covered them with fodder, saying to the judge afterward that he knew the Yankees would never get to that desolate island in the Dragon Swamp.

"But the Yankees, as everybody knew, were ubiquitous in Virginia during the war; and during Kilpatrick's raid through this county, they did visit the desolate island and fed their horses out of the very barn in which the records were concealed. But fortunately they did not go deep enough into the fodder to discover the boxes. So these valuable records were safely preserved."

Kilpatrick's "mounted devils," as they were called in the tidewater region, also went to the courthouse in Saluda looking for the county records. In 1916 P. T. Woodward's son W. W. Woodward wrote a letter to Morgan P. Robinson of the Virginia State Library as to what happened at the courthouse:

"My father, P. T. Woodward, was clerk of Middlesex County for forty years, beginning in 1852. My father had securely packed and removed the valuable books and papers during the war and concealed them in an out-of-the-way place in what is called the Dragon Swamp, which is [at] the headwaters of the Piankatank River. The Yankee troops broke into the office, and finding no valuable records, pulled down many old worthless papers, cut the strings and scattered them a foot deep on the brick floor."

Philemon T. Woodward saved the Middlesex County records from the Yankees by hiding them on an island in the swamp.

When Kilpatrick's "mounted devils" invaded the Middlesex County courthouse there were few records to be found. Clerk P. T. Woodward had hidden them away to keep the Yankees from burning them.

No one knows exactly where the papers were hidden. It is a good bet, though, that Woodward put them on Little Island in the Dragon Run. It is an island of about twenty acres, half of which is high ground located not far from Saluda and the courthouse. Woodward would not have had to carry them far and the island was owned by his family at that time. Also, if they were concealed in a barn, the papers would have been protected from the elements.

However, stories passed down have had the papers buried in several different places. One of the most interesting accounts, told by a granddaughter of a slave, said the papers were buried in a grave in the cemetery at Glebe Landing Baptist Church. It is not clear as to which location was the correct one, since the church has been on three different sites and all three sites were established before the Civil War. Two of the sites, however, were close to the Dragon Run. The church was organized in 1772, and the first building was located on a farm called the Glebe on the Rappahannock River. It was moved after a time to another site on the Dragon Run property of Henry Street and finally to its present one on Route 17, but not far from the Dragon. Since the story was passed down from slaves of the Street family, the location mentioned probably was the second site, if in fact it was one of the sites.

Woodward may have hidden papers in several different places so as not to lose them all if the Yankees were to stumble upon one of them. Another scenario could have been that he was planting decoys. In all oral accounts, it was stated that slaves were used to move the many boxes of records. Perhaps Woodward had not trusted anyone with the secret of the actual location of the papers and had buried several boxes filled with something other than the documents to help conceal the true location. If the Yankees were told a location of the papers, it might not have been the right one.

Also, it should be noted that southerners did everything possible to save family and community treasures from the Yankees. Woodward was not the only person burying papers. Other stories may have dealt with the hiding of church records or family papers. We will probably never know with certainty where the Middlesex

County papers were buried, but it should be understood that those living on the home front during the war were constantly in fear of the Yankees taking what they wanted—whether it was ham from the meat house, or the family silver, or papers that linked the family to some distant past.

In a 1988 letter to me, Mrs. Teresa Fields Bryant of Philadelphia wrote, "I was born in Middlesex County on May 21, 1901, the daughter of Mamie and John Fields. As a child I was raised by my grandfather, Robert Fields, whose land is in back of Union Shiloh Baptist Church. When he was in slavery he was a slave for a family by the name of Street at Waterview, Virginia.

"After the war he was a book salesman and he would nearly always take me with him. When we passed Glebe Landing Baptist Church he repeated what the coachman, named Old Jack, of the Street family had told him. Old Jack said that his master, some other men, and himself had buried some very important papers in a grave at old Glebe Landing Baptist Church. When it was heard the Yankees were marching through Middlesex, they buried the papers by the light of the moon and lantern and were all told by Mr. Street not to tell anyone where they were buried. Old Jack, however, told my grandfather."

One day when Teresa and her grandfather were passing the new church in a horse-drawn wagon, she asked her grandfather where the papers were buried. "I asked my grandfather to show me where old Glebe Landing Baptist Church was located and where the papers were buried and he said he would.

"We went past the new church and when we got a short distance down the road near to where my grandfather was going, a strange thing happened.

"Snip, our horse, stood up on his back legs with his front feet folded in as if someone had him by the bridle backing him back. My grandfather hit him but he would not go. I often think, even now, did the ghost of the coachman have him by the bridle or not? My grandfather would often say he wished he knew what was in those papers now that he could read.

"My grandfather finally calmed Snip down and we turned around because he would go no further no matter how hard my grandfather tried. When we got back out on the main road, my grandfather could hardly hold Snip back from galloping.

"We did not know for sure but I always thought that the papers were the ones from the courthouse."*

---

* Mrs. Bryant also shared this story in *Family Histories of Middlesex County, Virginia,* compiled and edited by Jessie M. De Busk, Charles L. Price, Jr., Louise E. Gray, and Dorothy M. Price.

16

A CHRISTMAS HAM

"Christmas morning, Mamma would make us cracklin' bread over the open fire. Everything was cooked in the fireplace then. We didn't have no stoves. We would put homemade butter and molasses all over the cracklin' bread. And a big ham, we'd always have a big ham and eat on it all week long," recalled Hallie Carr.

Hallie was born in 1885 in South Boston, Virginia. She was over one hundred years old when she related the following story to me.

There was a stillness in the air as a gentle snow fell softly to the ground. It was Christmas Eve 1864 and pressed against the windowpanes of the one-room, lofted shanty were eleven little black faces of the Hodgers family. They were bunched up watching the snow fall.

The chill winter air against the outside of the panes and the warm breath of the children on the inside frosted up the window so they were unable to see out. "I can't see the snow," complained one. "You're fogging up the window."

When one child tried to clear the panes by rubbing his shirt sleeve against it, the moisture smeared. "It's even worse now," screamed another youngster.

For just a moment, the spell of nature and the falling snow had taken their minds away from the suffering going on in a corner of

104

the little house. The children's mother, Mary Hodgers, was expecting her twelfth child and was in labor. May Frances, the local midwife, was getting ready to deliver another Hodgers into the world. She had delivered all eleven of the children in that same corner of the shanty.

The older children had heard the sounds of their mother in labor before, but her discomfort brought concern to the younger children.

"She'll be fine," said May Frances to the children as she took a bed sheet and draped it over a rope so the children could not see what was happening.

Delvin and Mary Hodgers were slaves on the Clark farm. They had heard that the war was just about over and were waiting to be told that they were free.

Several days before, Massa Clark had sent Delvin and two other slaves to town to pick up supplies. Delvin had not wanted to go because the baby was so close, but Massa Clark insisted and sent his slave master to make sure they did what they were supposed to do.

As the night lingered on, the children tried to sleep but their mother's cries kept them awake.

Suddenly, May Frances called to Jacob, the oldest, to come down from the loft. "Go get Doc Christian! Right now! Take the path to his house and run as fast as you can and tell him May Frances needs him quick."

"But, May Frances, Doc Christian is off fighting the Yankees," said Jacob.

"No, he ain't," said May Frances. "He came home last week. Now run as fast as you can and fetch him here. Tell him your mother needs him bad. It's life or death! He'll come!"

Into the snowy night, Jacob ran over the frozen path toward Doc's large farmhouse, a good mile from the little shanty. Doc Christian was a surgeon in the Confederate army but had come home because his mother was real sick. Jacob pushed himself to run as fast as he could along the narrow path. The winding track stretched through a long field, down to a foot bridge that crossed a little stream, and up a hill that took Jacob to Doc's lane.

When he got to Doc's house, he banged on the door as hard as he could. An old white-haired black man named Moses answered the door. Jacob had known Moses all his life.

"What do you want, Jacob?" asked old Moses.

"My mamma is real sick! May Frances said she needs Doc Christian or she will surely die. Please get him, Moses!" pleaded Jacob.

"What is it, Moses?" came a voice from the other room. It was Rebecca Christian, Doc's wife.

"It's a slave boy from over Massa Clark's," said Moses. "His mother needs Doc Christian bad."

Rebecca came to the door and saw the panic in the child's face. She sent Moses upstairs to get Doc and then went herself to get another servant to go and hitch up the buggy. Doc came down the stairs quickly with his bag in hand. "The buggy ready?" he asked.

"It's ready," said Rebecca with a large overcoat in her hands. She helped Doc into it and gave him a kiss.

"Come on, Jacob," said Moses. The three got into the buggy and quickly headed towards the Hodgers' slave shanty.

When they arrived, Doc went through the door first. May Frances explained the situation and the two went behind the curtain to attend to Mary, while Moses and Jacob sat down at the table to await the outcome.

Labor had started at suppertime and Mary had not had a chance to clear all the food from the table. A partially sliced ham was still in the center of the table.

Jacob went up in the loft to comfort the younger children and encourage them to sleep. The night seemed to last forever as Mary's cries continued on and on.

Suddenly, the family dog alerted Jacob and Moses that someone was coming. They could hear horses galloping down the road. "Maybe that's my daddy," said Jacob.

Then there was a bang on the door. When Moses opened the door, there were four white men standing there with rifles pointed at Moses and Jacob.

"Both of you get out here right now," yelled one. Moses and Jacob knew these men. They should have been off fighting the Yankees, but were too yellow to fight in any army. They stayed home and caused nothing but trouble for everyone.

"What were you doing on the path tonight, Jacob?" yelled one of the men. "I seen ya. You wasn't running from my smokehouse, was ya?"

Jacob answered that he had not been near the man's smokehouse. Suddenly one of the men spotted the ham on the table. "Oh, yeah? What the hell is that on the table? It's my ham and damn if those little darkies haven't eaten part of it," yelled the man. He rushed forward and smacked Jacob to the ground. Moses stepped forward to help Jacob and was hit with the butt of a rifle.

"What's going on out here?" screamed Doc Christian, who had heard the commotion.

"This little darkie stole my ham," said the man, surprised to see Doc.

"What ham?" asked Doc. He stepped outside, got Moses and Jacob to their feet, and helped them into the house.

"That one, right there on the table."

Doc stepped back onto the porch and said, "That's not your ham, boys."

"How do you know, Doc?"

"Because I just brought it over here myself, from my house." Doc then walked over to the table, took his pocketknife out, and carved off a big slice of meat. He walked back out to where the men were standing and ate it in front of them.

"Now, do you think I would eat after them?" he asked.

The men were satisfied that Doc had brought the partially eaten ham from home and they left.

When they were gone, Doc put his hand on top of Jacob's head and said, "Sorry, boy, but I didn't know any easier way to get rid of them."

That Christmas Eve, the Hodgers were blessed with a new baby boy. He was named Doc, after Doc Christian who had done some quick thinking to keep those four men from doing some real damage.

Young Doc would only be a slave for four short months. The war ended in April 1865 and the members of the Hodgers family were finally free.

Doc returned to the war before it ended and was at Appomattox for the surrender.

For many years thereafter, the Hodgers family received a salted ham from the smokehouse of Doc and Rebecca on Christmas Eve. It was a reminder to all of that Christmas Eve in 1864. When Doc Christian died some twenty years later, all the children of Mary and Delvin attended the funeral in honor of his passing.

17

THE BURNING OF
BARRICK'S MILL

In 1987 I recorded an interview with my maternal grandfather, Raymond Blake, who lived in the Topping area of Middlesex County, Virginia. He told me then the story of Henry Barrick, a miller who helped place several torpedoes in the path of a Yankee vessel and blow it to smithereens.

In 1996 Pat Perkinson shared with me a copy of a report of a Union expedition carried out by the Thirty-sixth U.S. Colored Infantry to find Barrick and his accomplices. My grandfather's recollections provide an interesting counterpoint to the Yankee expedition report.

"Henry Barrick owned a gristmill down on Barrick's Mill Pond near Syringa [Virginia]," recounted Blake. "There were men in the community who got tired of the Yankees stealing their best silver and cleaning out their meat houses so they joined the Confederate cause to give the Yanks a bit of their own medicine. They didn't go off to war, though. There were things at home they could do to hurt the Yankees, and they went about the task of doing so. Henry Barrick was one of these men.

"The Confederates provided torpedoes, and Barrick and others would anchor the explosives in the channel of the Rappahannock River where Yankee boats were coming and going. These torpedoes were anchored off Mill Creek and other places and were positioned just under the water so they could not be detected by those on the boats.

"At night Mr. Barrick and the others would sit up on the high bluffs of the Rappahannock and watch. And one night a Yankee vessel ran into one of the torpedoes and it blew the ship to smithereens. They say it lit up the whole sky.

"It was not long after this that the Yankees sent over a Negro regiment to find Mr. Barrick and the others. The Yankees caught some of the men and killed some but they didn't catch Mr. Barrick.

"They were so frustrated over not catching him that they burned his gristmill down. He later built it back and the mill operated there until the 1940s.

"One of the stories I heard as a boy was that times were really bad then and no one had any money. A woman in the neighborhood went to the mill, not knowing it had been destroyed. As she walked through the woods toward the mill, she spotted something on the ground. It was a fifty-dollar U.S. greenback that one of the Yankees had dropped. It must have been a good feeling to know that at least someone got paid for all the things the Yankees took."*

The following excerpt is from the May 11–14, 1864, expedition report of the Thirty-sixth U.S. Colored Infantry written by A. G. Draper, commander of the expedition. The task was to find and destroy torpedoes near the mouth of the Rappahannock River.

"I have the honor to report that in accordance with instructions from department headquarters, telegraphed May 11, 1864, I em-

---

* Perhaps the story my grandfather heard as a boy was the same as the one told by Virginia Revere of Wake concerning her grandmother, Mrs. Elizabeth Creighton Walker: "It was during the War Between the States and grandfather was in service of the Southern cause. Grandmother had the responsibility of caring for all their young children. One day, needing meal for her family, she went to the mill [Barrick's Mill]. While walking along, shielding her eyes from the sunlight, she spied an unusual item lying in her path. At her feet was a fifty-dollar bill! The previous day a band of Union cavalrymen had pillaged the neighborhood." From *Historic Buildings in Middlesex County, Virginia, 1650-1875*, by Louise E. Gray, page 41.

barked the same evening with 300 men of the 36th U.S. Colored Troops and 13 cavalry [from Point Lookout, Maryland] on board the transport steamer *Star* and the gun boat *Yankee*, to accompany Captain Hooker, of the Potomac flotilla, in an expedition to the mouth of the Rappahannock for the purpose of destroying torpedoes. The expedition returned to this post on the evening of the 14th, having been completely successful.

"We landed on the morning of May 12th at Mill Creek, exploded three torpedoes and raised two. Marched about two miles and burnt the mill of Mr. Henry Barrick, an accomplice of the men who placed the torpedoes, thence we marched across the peninsula, enclosed between the Rappahannock and Piankatank Rivers, divided into two detachments, and marched down two roads leading toward Stingray Point. About three miles farther down, at the point where these two roads unite, our detachments united. At this point we discovered four new torpedoes concealed in the *woods*, constructed with tin cases, each containing about 50 pounds of powder. Suspecting the presence of some small armed parties on the point, I threw out a line of skirmishers extending completely across the peninsula, a distance of about three miles, placed a reserve of infantry and the cavalry in the road, and ordered the skirmish line to advance to the extreme point. The ground being covered in most places with thick woods and underbrush, and intersected with creeks and swamps, it was almost impossible to maintain an unbroken line, and the progress of the skirmishers was necessarily difficult and slow. After advancing in this manner some two or three miles a small portion of the skirmishers on the right center, five or six in number, encountered a party of nine men, consisting of cavalry and marines, under command of B. G. Burley and John Maxwell, acting masters, C.S. Navy and although the colored infantry were entirely separated from their officers, they immediately attacked them. A brisk skirmish ensued. The blacks soon received a small reinforcement and succeeded in killing or capturing the entire party except one. Acting Master Maxwell and four others were killed. Acting Master Burley and a sergeant and corporal of cavalry were captured. Our loss was one man killed and two seriously and one slightly wounded. The wounded will probably all recover.

"This little affair was conducted wholly by the black men as no officers arrived until after the fight was over. The colored soldiers would have killed all the prisoners had they not been restrained by Sergeant Price, who is also colored.

"Acting Masters Burley and Maxwell were in command of the party which captured the steamer *Titan* at Cherrystone. Maxwell was formerly an officer in the U. S. Navy.

"I enclose the letter of instructions from the rebel Secretary of Navy under which these officers acted, also Burley's British protection and a pass from the rebel Secretary of War, dated March 30, 1864, for B. G. Burley, a citizen of Great Britain, to pass beyond the limits of the Confederate states, which documents appear to me to furnish evidence that Burley was expected to act as a spy.

"We passed the night of the 12th on the banks of Fishing Bay, reembarked in the morning, crossed the Piankatank to Milford Haven where we landed and marched to Mathews Court House, where we captured one rebel sergeant and one private, also 33 head of cattle and 22 serviceable horses and mules, with some wagons for the use of our contraband farm on the Patuxent [River].

"We passed the night of the 13th at Milford Haven.

"On the 14th reembarked with our captured property and returned to Point Lookout.

"The expedition accomplished the destruction or capture of nine torpedoes, burnt one mill, killed five of the enemy, captured five, including two acting masters in the Rebel Navy, captured 33 head of cattle, 22 horses and mules, and quite a number of vehicles of various descriptions. Our total loss was one man killed, two seriously and one slightly wounded."

18

TWO MEN WITH DIFFERENT FATES

Alonza Harrow and William Henry Norton are two men whose stories stand in strong contrast. The two men both came from the same community, known then as Sandy Bottom and today as Deltaville, Virginia. The community is located at the tip of the Middle Peninsula and in 1861 seemed far removed from the war that was looming between North and South. The war would, however, find its way to Sandy Bottom.

Randolph Norton of Charlotte, North Carolina, and Deltaville shared the next two stories with me. William Henry Norton was his grandfather, and he knew "ol' man 'Lonza" Harrow as a neighbor who lived down the lane when he was growing up.

Beneath the Bed

Snowball bushes were in full bloom in early spring of 1862. The shad and herring runs had begun, and fishermen had set their nets to harvest fish going upriver. Young Alonza Harrow was one of those fishermen who worked his nets near the mouth of the Piankatank River. He had learned the trade from his father; along with farming a few acres of land with the family mule, he was able to keep from starving to death.

113

Alonza owned no slaves. He could hardly read or write. In his few years of life, he had only left Sandy Bottom one time and that was on a trip by sailing vessel to Baltimore. He knew nothing of states' rights and all those patriotic callings that would send many a young lad to his grave. And while he had heard talk of a war coming, he never considered that he would have to be a part of it.

One day a group representing the recently formed government of the Confederate States of America came to Sandy Bottom to conscript men to fight against the North. They were going from house to house looking for eligible young men. Alonza and William Henry Norton both lived on Lover's Lane, a narrow oystershell lane that wound down to Jackson Creek, and both fit the bill.

It just so happened that Alonza's mother was out in the yard when the group came down Lover's Lane and turned towards William Henry's home place. She walked down and asked a neighbor what was going on.

"They've come to get our young men to go off and fight in a war," she was told.

"They ain't going to get my Alonza," she said to herself as she quickstepped back to her home.

Alonza was down by their dock working to untangle a fishnet when he saw his mother coming down the path. "What's the matter, Mamma?" he asked.

"They're coming for you, boy."

"Who's coming for me?"

"Some men who want you to go off and fight in a war. All you would do is get yourself killed for nothing."

"Where should I go?"

"Come on to the house. We'll hide you," said his mother. There was a rope bed with a goose-down mattress over it. His mother got Alonza to crawl between the mattress and the ropes and she covered him. Then she piled clothes all over the bed to make the men think she was doing some spring cleaning.

A short while later, two men came to the door and asked for Alonza.

Randolph Norton grew up on Lover's Lane in Deltaville, Virginia. He recalls the story of "ol' man 'Lonza" Harrow and his grandfather, William Henry Norton.

"He's out working the water," Alonza's mother said.

"Do you mind if we look around?" said one of the men.

"Not at all," she replied.

One man looked around the yard while the other looked in the house, but Alonza was not to be found.

Alonza Harrow lived out his life in Sandy Bottom and is buried in the local cemetery in what is today Deltaville. He spent his life scratching a living out of a few acres of land and catching a few fish.

A Father Dies

After leaving Alonza's house and checking several other homes on Lover's Lane, the two men came back to William Henry Norton's home. At the age of twenty-seven he was conscripted into the Confederate army and told to pack his clothes and ready himself to go off to war.

William Henry was married and had two little children at home. His wife, Evalina, and their young sons, Hervie and John, walked with him to the gate and watched as he, the two men, and several other young recruits walked away. It's hard to say what thoughts went through Evalina's head, but for certain she knew that this could well be the last time she would ever see her husband. And indeed it was.

William Henry went into the Twenty-seventh Virginia Cavalry. It was at the second battle of Cold Harbor in 1863 that he was shot dead, leaving his wife a widow and his two sons orphans.

One of his sons, Hervie, married Olivia Jane Ailsworth and they had eleven children. One of their sons is Randolph Norton, who kindly related the following story to me.

"In 1932, Daddy [Hervie Norton] and I visited the battlefield at Cold Harbor," said Randolph. "Daddy was in the seafood business and about this time the Depression was on and he didn't have anything to do. The oyster industry was shot.

"I had bought a new Chevrolet out here at Jerry Harrow's, a local car dealer. I traded in a 1927 Model A Ford with a rumble seat. I was teaching school out in West Virginia and had a little money. I was making $165 a month and, believe it or not, that was big money in the Depression.

"I said, 'Pa I'm going to Richmond. Would you want to go?'

"He said yes, which surprised me. Pa wasn't one to stray far from home. 'Isn't that close to Cold Harbor?' he asked. I said yes.

" 'Do you think we could stop by there? I've always wanted to see where my daddy died.'

" 'Sure Pa,' I said.

"Well, he went with me. We came back from Richmond that afternoon and we stopped at the battlefield and those old trenches were still deep. Some were filled with straw and debris. We climbed

This old shotgun house was the home of William Henry Norton in Deltaville, Virginia. He was conscripted by the Confederate States of America to fight for the South. He left two young sons and a wife behind when he was killed at the second battle of Cold Harbor.

over them and then Pa stopped and told me to take off my hat. We didn't know where William Henry was buried. We had always heard he was in a mass Confederate grave somewhere up here.

"Pa turned to me with tears in his eyes and told me to bow my head. He said a prayer that day for his slain father.

"He then went and dug up a maple tree and a pine tree. We took the trees home and he set the maple out in front of his house and the pine in the side yard as a memorial to his slain father."

The old Norton home place was torn down in 1996, but the maple and pine trees planted in 1932 by Hervie Norton as a tribute to his father are still standing.

19

RECOLLECTIONS FROM CHARLIE PALMER

My great-grandfather, Charles Henry Palmer, fought in the Fifty-fifth Infantry Division of Robert E. Lee's Army of Northern Virginia. The stories that follow were passed down from Charles Henry to his son (my great-uncle) Charlie Palmer, Jr.; to his grandson Henry Shepherd Chowning, Jr.; and to me, his great-grandson. As a child, I spent hours listening to family stories from my great-uncle. Charlie was mostly deaf and would often yell to hear himself talk. Many of his stories have stayed embedded in my mind even though years have passed and Charlie has long since gone to his Maker.

"Charles Henry Palmer, Sr., was sixteen years old in 1862 when he was conscripted to fight in the Confederate army. My grandfather, Alfred Palmer, had reached middle age by this time. The Confederate army was looking for any and all able-bodied men to help with the war effort. My grandfather had come from a wealthy family. His grandfather, David, had been a planter in lower Middlesex County in the late 1700s and had owned several large plantations. In 1824, my great-grandfather Opie inherited one of them.

"Alfred grew up on the plantation, but he didn't want to be a farmer. He wanted to go to town and make his own way. So, at an early age, he left and moved to Urbanna, where he would own and

Charlie Palmer was twenty-one years old in 1910 when this photo was taken. His father, Charles Henry Palmer, went off to fight in the Civil War when he was sixteen years old. Charlie recalled the war stories of his father and passed them down to his nephew, Henry Shepherd Chowning, and great-nephew, Larry Shepherd Chowning.

operate Palmer's Steamboat Wharf along with several other commercial enterprises.

"One of those enterprises was part ownership of the first bridge going across Urbanna Creek. You see, the county seat of Middlesex County had been in Urbanna since 1748, but by the 1850s the often-slow ferry across Urbanna Creek was inconvenient for citizens coming from the lower portion of the county.

"My grandfather fought hard to keep the county seat in Urbanna because he felt it was important to his business and to the town as a whole. However, an act was passed on March 8, 1849, for there to be a vote to determine if the courthouse should be moved to a more central location. In June, it was voted to move the courthouse to Saluda. The deciding vote, it is said, was cast by a bitter opponent of the Urbanna location who was brought on a stretcher to the courthouse to cast his vote.

"This upset my grandfather, so around 1855 he and several businessmen in town had a toll bridge built across the creek to assure that people could easily access Urbanna.

"This was to eventually lead to several confrontations in the early years of the Confederacy with the government in Richmond. As the war progressed, southern troops would use the bridge and refuse to pay the toll. As they refused, others also refused. This frustrated my grandfather.

"I'm telling you all this to try and explain the reasoning behind his decision in 1862 to have his teenage son substitute for himself in the southern army. By this time, my father's mother, Matilda Bailey Chowning Palmer, had passed and there was no mother to beg for her son to be spared.

"When the Confederates came looking for more soldiers Alfred Palmer told the men he had a sixteen-year-old son and asked if his son could go in his place. They agreed. So my father packed up a few belongings and became a soldier at a youthful age.

"He joined the Fifty-fifth Virginia Infantry, which was mostly composed of Middlesex men. Captain of the Middlesex Southerners was Dr. William S. Christian, who was affectionately called 'Captain Billy.'

"My father had a stormy experience in the war. In one of his first battles—the Battle of Frazier's Farm—he was shot in the jaw. Captain Billy found him and administered first aid to him. Then he and others carried him off the battlefield to a surgeon's tent where a doctor removed the bullet. Before starting, the surgeon took a bullet from his pouch and told my father to open his mouth. When he did, the doctor put the bullet between his teeth and told him to bite down hard. My father passed out. When he awoke, the bullet that had been stuck between his teeth was in his shirt pocket. He later brought it home and I have it to this day. His teeth marks can still be seen in it.

"After being shot, he came home for a while and went back after a short recovery. Towards the end of the war, he was captured near Richmond and placed in prison at Point Lookout, Maryland. There he stayed until the end of the war.

"Prisoners were released from Point Lookout by alphabetical order of their last name. He had to wait until the Ps came up before he was released.

"When he arrived in Urbanna, several of my grandfather's former slaves were still living at the home place. Opie Palmer had died in 1845 and left my grandfather five slaves.

"When my father walked through the door, he was covered in lice, so two of the Negroes went with him down to Urbanna Creek and they scrubbed him down in the salt water until he was clean.

"The war had taken its toll on the town. My grandfather's businesses had all collapsed, and there was very little food around. To help feed the family, my father took the family punt [a small skiff with blunted ends on bow and stern] and sculled out to the mouth of Urbanna Creek to tong oysters. As he tonged, he kept bringing up coal mixed in with the oysters.

"He was later to learn that several Yankee schooners laden with coal had been sunk off the mouth of the creek.* That winter, the townspeople went out and tonged oysters to eat and coal to keep their fires burning.

"Shortly after the war, my father left and went to New York State where he stayed for seven years. While there, he learned the carpentry trade. In 1872, he came home, built himself a small shop, and was the town carpenter until his death. He married Nannie Sadler in 1878 and they had three children. I was born in 1889, the youngest of his children.

"He built and designed the Baptist church, built the old Masonic lodge, his own house that I live in today, and several other houses in town.

"My father died in 1904 and was buried at Glebe Landing Baptist Church near Laneview, Virginia."

The home that Charles Henry Palmer began in 1875 and completed in 1878 is today the home of the present writer, his great-grandson, Larry S. Chowning. Legend has it that Nannie Sadler refused to marry Charles until he completed their house. For whatever reason, it took him three years.

---

* Three Union schooners were captured off Gwynn Island in Mathews County in August 1863 by Confederate forces led by John Taylor Wood. The schooners were hauling coal from Baltimore to Maine. Wood and his small band of men had earlier captured two Yankee gunboats anchored off Stingray Point. The gunboats, named *Reliance* and *Satellite*, were used by Wood to commandeer the schooners. Wood brought the three vessels—*Golden Rod, Coquette,* and *Two Brothers*—to the mouth of Urbanna Creek, took off as much coal and other items as he could, and then sank the vessels. It is a good bet that the coal tonged up from the bottom of the creek by my great-grandfather came from these ships. From *John Taylor Wood: Sea Ghost of the Confederacy,* by Royce Gordon Shingleton, pp. 84–87.

INDEX

Chowning, Henry Shepherd, Jr., 3, 119–20
Chowning, James Henry, 4
Chowning, Larry Shepherd, 120, 123
Chowning, Carroll, Sr. (Uncle Carroll), xi, 3–4, 8–9
Christ Church parish, 3
Christian, Captain Billy, xi, 60–1, 122
Christian, Doc, 105–8
Christian, Judge Joseph, 98
Christian, Rebecca, 106, 108
Church of England, 4
Church View, Virginia, 65
Clifton, 56–7
Collins, John, 90–1, 93–4, 96
Confederate money, 34–5
Copper, John (Cop), 49–50, 52
Coquette (schooner), 123
Corbin Hall, 37, 39, 49–50, 52
Corbin, Mutt, 49–53
Corbin, Russell, 49–50, 52
Corbins, 26, 38
Custis Farm, 66
Custis, Master, 66–70

Dahlgren's Corner, 43
Dahlgren, Ulric, 43–4, 47
Davies, Suzy, 87
Deer Chase Farm, 32
Deltaville, Virginia, 63, 64, 71–4, 113, 115–7
Depression, 116–7
Dickens, Elizabeth Bolling, 14
Dickerson, Fielding Lewis, 58, 60
Dickerson, William B., 25–6, 28–30, 48, 53, 66
Dover, Sam, 66–8
Dragon Run Swamp, 56, 98, 101
Draper, A. G., 110
Dyer Creek, 33

Ellyson, Josie Henley, 80–1
Emancipation, 27
Essex County, Virginia, 12–3, 39, 58, 69
Eubank, James Archer, 57
Eubank, Joseph C., 25, 27–9, 37–9, 40–2

Eubank, Lucy, 25–7, 37–42
Eubank, Massa Dan, 39
Eubank, Mrs., 57
Ewell, Mary Steed, 81

Falmouth Heights, 17
Falmouth, Virginia, 14–6
Ferneyhough, Charles, 57
Ferneyhough, Salome Stiff, 57
Fields, Birdie, 66–70
Fields, Black Will, 66–70
Fields, John, 102
Fields, Mamie, 102
Fields, Robert, 70, 102–3
Fishing Bay, 63, 72–3, 112
Flood, Jerry, 87
Ford's Theater, 24
Forest, The, 56
Frances, May, 105–6
Fredericksburg, Virginia, 14, 16–8, 21–2

Gaskins, Fred, 64
Georgia, 32, 91
Glebe, 3–7
Glebe Landing Baptist Church, 37–8, 101–2, 123
Gloucester County, Virginia, 87
Gloucester Point, Virginia, 43, 47, 87
Golden Rod (schooner), 123
Grant, General Ulysses S., 65
Grape Bush, 35
Gray, Louise E., 110
Greys Point, 54
Grimsby Farm, 31–2
Gwynn Island, Virginia, 123

Harpers Ferry, West Virginia, 28
Harrow, Alonza, 113–6
Harrow, Jerry, 116
Hartwood Presbyterian Church, 18
Hartwood, Virginia, 14–6, 18–9
Henley, Todd, 83
Henley, William Todd, Jr., 80, 86
Hewick, 60–2
Hillsborough, 80–7